Dinosaurs

Is there a biblical explanation?

WHAT HAPPENED TO THE DINOSAURS? • DID DINOSAURS TURN INTO BIRDS? • WHY DON'T WE FIND HUMAN AND DINOSAUR FOSSILS TOGETHER? • DINOSAUR KILLER • ALIVE AFTER BABEL?

A POCKET GUIDE TO . . .

Dinosaurs

Is there a biblical explanation?

Petersburg, Kentucky, USA

Reprinted May 2016

ISBN: 978-1-60092-301-2

Printed in China

AnswersInGenesis.org

Table of Contents

Introduction

Dinosaurs have captured the imagination of people through-out history. Dinosaurs are mysterious creatures known primar-ily from the fossilized bones that we find. Scientists who study the fossils attempt to reconstruct these creatures that ranged from the size of a rat to the largest living animals to ever roam the planet. How they interpret the fossil evidence has led to much controversy.

Starting from the assumption that the earth is billions of years old, most scientists believe dinosaurs lived millions of years ago, dying out over 60 million years ago. Detailed explanations of how they hunted, ate, cared for their young, and changed through the millenia are offered. We must ask how accurate these interpreta-tions are in light of the scant evidence that is available.

What does the Bible teach when it comes to dinosaurs? Though the Bible doesn't use the word *dinosaur*, the descriptions in Job and other books sound a lot like dinosaurs we know from the fossil deposits. The biblical view has dinosaurs—land animals—created on Day Six of the Creation Week. This means that they would have lived at the same time as man, a notion contrary to the evolutionary explanation.

Is there evidence that dinosaurs lived alongside man? Are the birds feeding in your backyard really dinosaurs? What can we know from the fossil evidence? These questions and others will be answered from the perspective we gain from God's Word—the Bible.

What Really Happened to the Dinosaurs?

by Ken Ham

Dinosaurs are used more than almost anything else to indoctrinate children and adults in the idea of millions of years of earth history. However, the Bible gives us a framework for explaining dinosaurs in terms of thousands of years of history, including the mystery of when they lived and what happened to them. Two key texts are Genesis 1:24–25 and Job 40:15–24.

Are dinosaurs a mystery?

Many think that the existence of dinosaurs and their demise is shrouded in such mystery that we may never know the truth about where they came from, when they lived, and what happened to them. However, dinosaurs are only a mystery *if* you accept the evolutionary story of their history.

According to evolutionists:

Dinosaurs first evolved around 235 million years ago, long before man evolved.[1] No human being ever lived with dinosaurs. Their history is recorded in the fossil layers on earth, which were deposited over millions of years. They were so successful as a group of animals that they eventually ruled the earth. However, around 65 million years ago, something happened to change all of this—the dinosaurs disappeared. Most evolutionists believe some sort of cataclysmic event, such as an asteroid impact, killed them. But many evolutionists claim that some dinosaurs evolved into birds, and thus they are not extinct but are flying around us even today.[2]

There is no mystery surrounding dinosaurs if you accept the Bible's totally different account of dinosaur history.

According to the Bible:

On the basis of the Bible's history, and what we observe in today's world, we can outline seven "ages" that apply to dinosaurs.

Dinosaurs first existed around 6,000 years ago.[3] God formed the dinosaurs, along with the other land animals, on Day Six of the Creation Week (Genesis 1:20–25, 31). Adam and Eve were also made on Day Six—so dinosaurs lived at the same time as people, not separated by eons of time.

Like all other animals and man, dinosaurs originally ate only fruits and vegetables (Genesis 1:29–30). They did not start eating other animals until after the Fall of man. Man and animals were not afraid of each other. This was the fearless age.

When Adam disobeyed His Creator, death, bloodshed, and suffering entered the world (Romans 5:12, 14; 1 Corinthians 15:21–22). At some point after this, dinosaurs and other animals began to eat each other. Everything was affected by the Fall.

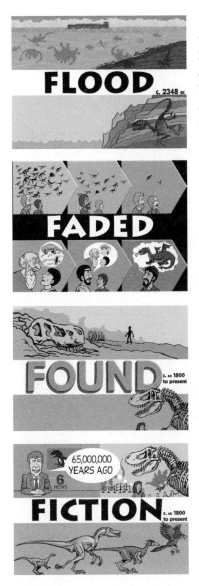

Representatives of all the kinds of air-breathing land animals, including the dinosaur kinds, went aboard Noah's Ark. All those left outside the Ark died in the cataclysmic circumstances of the Flood, and many of their remains became fossils.

After the Flood, around 4,300 years ago, the remnant of the land animals, including dinosaurs, came off the Ark and lived in the present world, along with people. Because of sin, the judgments of the Curse and the Flood have greatly changed the earth. Post-Flood climatic change, lack of food, disease, and man's activities caused many types of animals to become extinct. The dinosaurs, like many other creatures, died out, and man's memory of these great creatures faded.

Ancient people found bones from creatures that belonged to a group of land animals no longer alive on earth. In the 1800s, the term *dinosaur* was created for these creatures.

Today, man has invented all kinds of stories about dinosaurs: they ruled the earth over 60 million years ago; they died out when an asteroid struck the earth; they evolved into birds, etc. And today these fictional stories are taught as truth.

Why such different views?

How can there be such totally different explanations for dinosaurs? Whether one is an evolutionist or accepts the Bible's account of history, the evidence for dinosaurs is *the same*. All scientists have the same facts—they have the same world, the same fossils, the same living creatures, the same universe.

If the "facts" are the same, then how can the explanations be so different? The reason is that scientists have only the present—dinosaur fossils exist only in the present—but scientists are trying to connect the fossils in the present to the past. They ask, "What happened in history to bring dinosaurs into existence, wipe them out, and leave many of them fossilized?"[4]

The science that addresses such issues is known as *historical* or

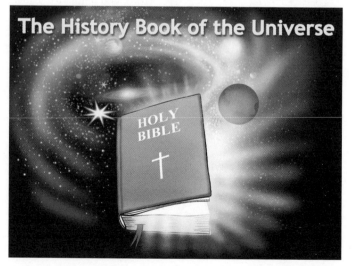

The History Book of the Universe

HOLY BIBLE

origins science, and it differs from the *operational science* that gives us computers, inexpensive food, space exploration, electricity, and the like. Origins science deals with the past, which is not accessible to direct experimentation, whereas operational science deals with how the world works in the here and now, which, of course, is open to repeatable experiments. Because of difficulties in reconstructing the past, those who study fossils (paleontologists) have diverse views on dinosaurs.[5] As has been said, "Paleontology (the study of fossils) is much like politics: passions run high, and it's easy to draw very different conclusions from the same set of facts."[6]

A paleontologist who believes the record in the Bible, which claims to be the Word of God,[7] will come to different conclusions than an atheist who rejects the Bible. Willful denial of God's Word (2 Peter 3:3–7) lies at the root of many disputes over historical science.

Many people think the Bible is just a book about religion or salvation. It is much more than this. The Bible is the History Book of the Universe and tells us the future destiny of the universe as well. It gives us an account of when time began, the main events of history, such as the entrance of sin and death into the world, the time when the *whole* surface of the globe was destroyed by water, the giving of different languages at the Tower of Babel, the account of the Son of God coming as a man, His death and Resurrection, and the new heavens and earth to come.

Ultimately, there are only two ways of thinking: starting with the revelation from God (the Bible) as foundational to *all* thinking (including biology, history, and geology), resulting in a *Christian worldview*; or starting with man's beliefs (for example, the evolutionary story) as foundational to all thinking, resulting in a *secular worldview*.

Most Christians have been indoctrinated through the media and education system to think in a secular way. They tend to take secular thinking to the Bible, instead of using the Bible to *build* their thinking (Romans 12:1–2; Ephesians 4:20–24).

Secular history   Dinosaurs   Biblical history

The Bible says, "The fear of the Lord is the beginning of knowledge" (Proverbs 1:7) and "the fear of the Lord is the beginning of wisdom" (Proverbs 9:10).

If one begins with an evolutionary view of history (for which there were no witnesses or written record), then this way of thinking will be used to explain the evidence that exists in the present. Thus, we have the evolutionary explanation for dinosaurs above.

But if one begins with the biblical view of history from the written record of an eyewitness (God) to all events of history, then a totally different way of thinking, based on this, will be used to explain the *same* evidence. Thus, we have the biblical explanation given above.

Dinosaur history

Fossil bones of dinosaurs are found around the world. Many of these finds consist of just fragments of bones, but some nearly complete skeletons have been found. Scientists have been able to describe many different types of dinosaurs based on distinctive characteristics, such as the structure of the skull and limbs.[8]

Where did dinosaurs come from?

The Bible tells us that God created different kinds of land animals on Day 6 of Creation Week (Genesis 1:24–25). Because dinosaurs were land animals, this must have included the dinosaur kinds.[9]

Evolutionists claim that dinosaurs evolved from some reptile that had originally evolved from amphibians. But they cannot point to any clear transitional (in-between) forms to substantiate their argument. Dinosaur family trees in evolutionary books show many distinct types of dinosaurs, but only hypothetical lines join them up to some common ancestor. The lines are dotted because there is *no* fossil evidence. Evolutionists simply cannot prove their belief in a nondinosaur ancestor for dinosaurs.

What did dinosaurs look like?

Scientists generally do not dig up a dinosaur with all its flesh intact. Even if they found *all* the bones, they still would have less than 40 percent of the animal to work out what it originally looked like. The bones do not tell the color of the animal, for example, although some fossils of skin impressions have been found, indicating the skin texture. As there is some diversity of color among reptiles living today, dinosaurs may have varied greatly in color, skin texture, and so on.

When reconstructing dinosaurs from bony remains, scientists make all kinds of guesses and often disagree. For example, debate has raged about whether dinosaurs were warm- or cold-blooded. It is even difficult to tell whether a dinosaur was male or female from its bones. There is much speculation about such things.

Sometimes scientists make mistakes in their reconstructions, which need correction when more bones are found. For instance, the famous *Brontosaurus* is not in newer dinosaur dictionaries. The original "discoverer" put the wrong head on a skeleton of a dinosaur that had already been named *Apatosaurus*.[10]

Who discovered dinosaurs?

Secular books would tell you that the first discovery of what later were called dinosaurs was in 1677 when Dr. Robert Plot found bones so big they were thought to belong to a giant elephant or a giant human.[11]

In 1822, Mary Anne Mantell went for a walk along a country road in Sussex, England. According to tradition, she found a stone that glittered in the sunlight and showed it to her fossil-collecting husband. Dr. Mantell, a physician, noticed that the stone contained a tooth similar to, but much larger than, that of modern reptiles. He concluded that it belonged to some extinct giant plant-eating reptile with teeth like an iguana. In 1825 he named the owner of the tooth *Iguanodon* (iguana tooth). It was Dr. Mantell who began to popularize the "age of reptiles."[12]

From a biblical perspective, however, the time of the above discoveries was actually the time when dinosaurs were *rediscovered*. Adam discovered dinosaurs when he first observed them.

When did dinosaurs live?

Evolutionists claim dinosaurs lived millions of years ago. But it is important to realize that when they dig up a dinosaur bone it does not have a label attached showing its date. Evolutionists obtain their dates by *indirect*

dating methods that other scientists question, and there is much evidence against the millions of years.[13]

Does God tell us when He made *Tyrannosaurus rex*? Many would say no. But the Bible states that God made all things in six normal days. He made the land animals, including dinosaurs, on Day 6 (Genesis 1:24–25), so they date from around 6,000 years ago—the approximate date of creation obtained by adding up the years in the Bible.[14] So, since *T. rex* was a land animal and God made all the land animals on Day 6, then God made *T. rex* on Day 6.

Furthermore, from the Bible we see that there was no death, bloodshed, disease, or suffering before sin.[15] If one approaches Genesis to Revelation consistently, interpreting Scripture with Scripture, then death and bloodshed of man and animals came into the world only *after* Adam sinned. The first death of an animal occurred when God shed an animal's blood in the Garden of Eden and clothed Adam and Eve (Genesis 3:21). This was also a picture of the Atonement—foreshadowing Christ's blood that was to be shed for us. Thus, there could *not* have been bones of dead animals before sin—this would undermine the gospel.

This means that the dinosaurs must have died after sin entered the world, not before. Dinosaur bones could *not* be millions of years old because Adam lived only thousands of years ago.

Does the Bible mention dinosaurs?

If people saw dinosaurs, you would think that ancient historical writings, such as the Bible, should mention them. The King James Version was first translated in 1611.[16] Some people think that because the word "dinosaur" is not found in this or other translations, the Bible does not mention dinosaurs.

It was not until 1841, however, that the word "dinosaur" was invented.[17] Sir Richard Owen, a famous British anatomist and first superintendent of the British Museum (and a staunch anti-

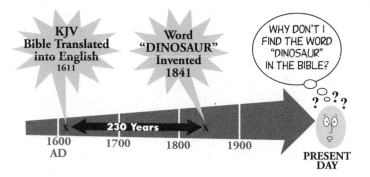

Darwinist), on viewing the bones of *Iguanodon* and *Megalosaurus*, realized these represented a unique group of reptiles that had not yet been classified. He coined the term "dinosaur" from Greek words meaning "terrible lizard."[18]

Thus, one would not expect to find the word "dinosaur" in the King James Bible—the word did not exist when the translation was done.

Is there another word for "dinosaur"? There are *dragon* legends from around the world. Many dragon descriptions fit the characteristics of specific dinosaurs. Could these actually be accounts of encounters with what we now call dinosaurs?

Just as Flood legends are based on a real global Flood (Flood of Noah)—dragon legends are possibly based on actual encounters with real animals that today we call dinosaurs. Many of these land-dragon descriptions do fit with what we know about dinosaurs.

In Genesis 1:21, the Bible says, "And God created the great sea monsters and every living creature that moves, with which the waters swarmed, after their kind." The Hebrew word here for "sea monsters" ("whales" in KJV) is the word translated elsewhere as "dragon" (Hebrew: *tannin*). So, in the first chapter of the first book of the Bible, God may be describing the great sea dragons (sea-dwelling, dinosaur-type animals) that He created.

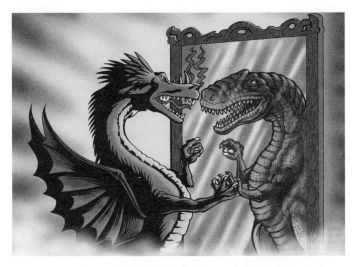

There are other Bible passages about dragons that lived in the sea: "the dragons in the waters" (Psalm 74:13), "and he shall slay the dragon that is in the sea" (Isaiah 27:1). Though the word "dinosaur" strictly refers to animals that lived on the land, the sea reptiles and flying reptiles are often grouped with the dinosaurs. The sea dragons could have included dinosaur-type animals such as the *Mosasaurus*.[19]

Job 41 describes a great animal that lived in the sea, Leviathan, that even breathed fire. This "dragon" may have been something like the mighty 40 ft. (12 m) *Sarcosuchus imperator* (Super Croc),[20] or the 82 ft. (25 m) *Liopleurodon*.

There is also mention of a flying serpent in the Bible: the "fiery flying serpent" (Isaiah 30:6). This could be a reference to one of the pterodactyls, which are popularly thought of as flying dinosaurs, such as the *Pteranodon*, *Rhamphorhynchus*, or *Ornithocheirus*.[21]

Not long after the Flood, God was showing a man called Job how great He was as Creator, by reminding Job of the largest land animal He had made:

Look now at the behemoth, which I made along with you; he eats grass like an ox. See now, his strength is in his hips, and his power is in his stomach muscles. He moves his tail like a cedar; the sinews of his thighs are tightly knit. His bones are like beams of bronze, his ribs like bars of iron. He is the first of the ways of God; only He who made him can bring near His sword (Job 40:15–19).

The phrase "first of the ways of God" suggests this was the largest land animal God had made. So what kind of animal was "behemoth"?

Bible translators, not being sure what this beast was, often transliterated the Hebrew, and thus the word *behemoth* (e.g., KJV, NKJV, NASB, NIV). However, in many Bible commentaries and Bible footnotes, "behemoth" is said to be "possibly the hippopotamus or elephant."[22] Some Bible versions actually translate "behemoth" this way.[23] Besides the fact that the elephant and hippo were *not* the largest land animals God made (some of the dinosaurs far eclipsed these), this description does not make sense, since the tail of behemoth is compared to the large cedar tree (Job 40:17).

Now an elephant's tiny tail (or a hippo's tail that looks like a flap of skin) is quite unlike a cedar tree. Clearly, the elephant and the hippo could not possibly be "behemoth."

No *living* creature comes close to this description. However, behemoth is very much like *Brachiosaurus*, one of the large dinosaurs.

Are there other ancient records of dinosaurs?

In the film *The Great Dinosaur Mystery*,[24] a number of dragon accounts are presented:

- A Sumerian story dating back to 2000 BC or earlier tells of a hero named Gilgamesh, who, when he went to fell cedars in a remote forest, encountered a huge vicious dragon that he slew, cutting off its head as a trophy.

- When Alexander the Great (c. 330 BC) and his soldiers marched into India, they found that the Indians worshipped huge hissing reptiles that they kept in caves.

- China is renowned for its dragon stories, and dragons are prominent on Chinese pottery, embroidery, and carvings.

- England and several other cultures retain the story of St. George, who slew a dragon that lived in a cave.

- There is the story of a tenth-century Irishman who wrote of his encounter with what appears to have been a *Stegosaurus*.

In the 1500s, a European scientific book, *Historia Animalium*, listed several living animals that we would call dinosaurs. A well-known naturalist of the time, Ulysses Aldrovandus, recorded an encounter between a peasant named Baptista and a dragon whose description fits that of the small dinosaur *Tanystropheus*. The encounter was on May 13, 1572, near Bologna in Italy, and the peasant killed the dragon.

Petroglyphs (drawings carved on rock) of dinosaurlike creatures have also been found.[25]

In summary, people down through the ages have been very familiar with dragons. The descriptions of these animals fit with what we know about dinosaurs. The Bible mentions such creatures, even ones that lived in the sea and flew in the air. There is a tremendous amount of other historical evidence that such creatures have lived beside people.

What do the bones say?

There is also physical evidence that dinosaur bones are not millions of years old. Scientists from Montana State University found *T. rex* bones that were not totally fossilized. Sections of the bones were like fresh bone and contained what seems to be blood cells and hemoglobin. If these bones really were tens of millions of years old, then the blood cells and hemoglobin would have totally disintegrated.[26] Also, there should not be "fresh" bones if they were really millions of years old.[27] A report by these scientists stated the following:

> A thin slice of *T. rex* bone glowed amber beneath the lens of my microscope . . . . The lab filled with murmurs of amazement, for I had focused on something inside the vessels that none of us had ever noticed before: tiny round objects, translucent red with a dark center ... . Red blood cells? The shape and location suggested them, but blood cells are mostly water and couldn't possibly have stayed preserved in the 65-million-year-old *tyrannosaur* . . . . The bone sample that had us so excited came from a beautiful, nearly complete specimen of *Tyrannosaurus rex* unearthed in 1990 . . . . When the team brought the dinosaur into the lab, we noticed that some parts deep inside the long bone of the leg had not completely fossilized ... . So far, we think that all of this evidence supports the notion that our slices of *T. rex* could contain preserved heme and hemoglobin fragments. But more work needs to be done before we are confident enough to come right out and say, "Yes, this *T. rex* has blood compounds left in its tissues."[28]

Unfossilized duck-billed dinosaur bones have been found on the North Slope in Alaska.[29] Also, creation scientists collected such (unfossilized) frozen dinosaur bones in Alaska.[30]

Evolutionists would not say that these bones had stayed frozen for the many millions of years since these dinosaurs supposedly died out (according to evolutionary theory). Yet the bones could not have survived for the millions of years unmineralized. This is a puzzle to those who believe in an "age of dinosaurs" millions of years ago, but not to someone who builds his thinking on the Bible.

What did dinosaurs eat and how did they behave?

Movies like *Jurassic Park* and *The Lost World* portray most dinosaurs as aggressive meat-eaters. But the mere presence of sharp teeth does *not* tell you how an animal behaved or necessarily what food it ate—only what kind of teeth it had (for ripping food and the like). However, by studying fossil dinosaur dung (coprolite), scientists have been able to determine the diet of some dinosaurs.[31]

Originally, before sin, *all* animals, including the dinosaurs, were vegetarian. Genesis 1:30 states, "And to every beast of the earth, and to every bird of the air, and to every thing that creeps upon the earth, which has life, I have given every green herb for food: and it was so."

This means that even *T. rex*, before sin entered the world, ate only plants. Some people object to this by pointing to the big teeth that a large *T. rex* had, insisting they must have been used for attacking animals. However, just because an animal has big, sharp teeth does not mean it eats meat. It just means it has big, sharp teeth![32]

Many animals today have sharp teeth but are basically vegetarian. The giant panda has sharp teeth like a meat-eater's, but it eats bamboo. Perhaps the panda's teeth were beautifully designed to eat bamboo. To explain why a giant panda has teeth like a meat-eaters today, yet eats bamboo, evolutionists have to say that the giant panda evolved as a meat eater, and then switched to bamboo.[33]

Different species of bats variously eat fruit, nectar, insects, small animals, and blood, but their teeth do not clearly indicate what they eat.[34] Bears have teeth with carnivore features, but some bears are vegetarian, and many, if not most, are mainly vegetarian.

Before sin, God described the world as "very good" (Genesis 1:31). Some cannot accept this concept of perfect harmony because of the food chain that they observe in today's world. However, one cannot look at the sin-cursed world and the resultant death and struggle, and use this to reject the Genesis account of history. Everything has changed because of sin. That's why Paul describes the present creation as "groaning" (Romans 8:22). One must look through the Bible's "eyes" to understand the world.[35]

Some argue that people or animals would have been hurt even in an ideal world. They contend that even before sin, Adam or an animal could have stood on small creatures or scratched himself on a branch. Now these sorts of situations are true of today's fallen world—the present world is not perfect; it is suffering from the effects of the Curse (Romans 8:22). One cannot look at the Bible through the world's eyes and insist that the world before sin was just like the world we see today. We do not know what a perfect world, continually restored and totally upheld by God's power (Colossians 1:17; Hebrews 1:3), would have been like— we have never experienced perfection (only Adam and Eve did before sin).

We do get little glimpses from Scripture, however; in Deuteronomy 8:4, 29:5 and Nehemiah 9:21, we are told that when the Israelites wandered in the desert for 40 years, their clothes and shoes did not wear out, nor did their feet swell. When God upholds things perfectly, wearing out or being hurt in any way is not even an option.

Think of Shadrach, Meshach, and Abednego (Daniel 3:26–27). They came out of the fire without even the smell of smoke on them. Again, when the Lord upholds perfectly, being hurt is not possible. In a perfect world, before sin and the Curse, God would have upheld everything, but in this cursed world, things run down. Many commentators believe the description in Isaiah 11:6–9 of the wolf and lamb, and the lion that eats straw like an ox, is a picture of the new earth in the future restoration (Acts 3:21) when there will be no more curse or death (Revelation 21:1, 22:3). The animals described are living peacefully as vegetarians (this is also the description of the animal world before sin—Genesis 1:30). Today's world has been changed dramatically because of sin and the Curse. The present food chain and animal behavior (which also changed after the Flood—Genesis 9:2–3) cannot be used as a basis for interpreting the Bible—the Bible explains why the world is the way it is.

In the beginning, God gave Adam and Eve dominion over the animals: "Then God blessed them, and God said to them, 'Be fruitful and multiply; fill the earth and subdue it; have dominion over the fish of the sea, over the birds of the air, and over every living thing that moves on the earth'" (Genesis 1:28). Looking at today's world, we are reminded of Hebrews 2:8: "For in that He put all in subjection under him, He left nothing that is not put under him. But now we do not yet see all things put under him." Man's relationship with all things changed because of sin—they are not "under him" as they were originally.

Most people, including most Christians, tend to observe the world as it is today, with all its death and suffering, and then take that observation to the Bible and interpret it in that light. But we are sinful, fallible human beings, observing a sin-cursed world (Romans 8:22); and thus, we need to start with divine revelation, the Bible, to begin to understand.

So how did fangs and claws come about? Dr. Henry Morris, a founding figure in the modern creation movement, states:

Whether such structures as fangs and claws were part of their original equipment, or were recessive features which only became dominant due to selection processes later, or were mutational features following the Curse, or exactly what, must await further research.[36]

After sin entered the world, everything changed. Maybe some animals started eating each other at this stage. By the time of Noah, God described what had happened this way: "So God looked upon the earth, and indeed it was corrupt; for all flesh had corrupted their way on the earth" (Genesis 6:12).

Also, after the Flood, God changed the behavior of animals. We read, "And the fear of you and the dread of you shall be on every beast of the earth, on every bird of the air, on all that move on the earth, and on all the fish of the sea. They are given into your hand" (Genesis 9:2). Thus, man would find it much more difficult to carry out the dominion mandate given in Genesis 1:28.

Why do we find dinosaur fossils?

Fossil formation requires a sudden burial. When an animal dies, it usually gets eaten or decays until there is nothing left. To form a fossil, unique conditions are required to preserve the animal and replace it with minerals, etc.

Evolutionists once claimed that the fossil record was formed slowly as animals died and were gradually covered by sediment. But they have acknowledged more recently that the fossil record must involve catastrophic processes.[37] To form the billions of fossils worldwide, in layers sometimes kilometers thick, the organisms, by and large, must have been buried quickly. Many evolutionists now say the fossil record formed quickly, in spurts interspersed by millions of years.

According to the Bible, as time went on, earth became full of wickedness, so God determined that He would send a global

Flood "to destroy from under heaven all flesh in which is the breath of life" (Genesis 6:17).

God commanded Noah to build a very large boat into which he would take his family and representatives of every kind of land-dwelling, air-breathing animal (that God Himself would choose and send to Noah, Genesis 6:20). This must have included two of each kind of dinosaur.

How did dinosaurs fit on the Ark?

Many people think of dinosaurs as large creatures that would never have fit into the Ark.

But the average size of a dinosaur, based on the skeletons found over the earth, is about the size of a sheep.[38] Indeed, many dinosaurs were relatively small. For instance, *Struthiomimus* was the size of an ostrich, and *Compsognathus* was no bigger than a rooster. Only a few dinosaurs grew to extremely large sizes (e.g., *Brachiosaurus* and *Apatosaurus*), but even they were not as large as the largest animal in the world today, the blue whale. (Reptiles have the potential to grow as long as they live. Thus, the large dinosaurs were probably very old ones.)

Dinosaurs laid eggs, and the biggest fossil dinosaur egg found is about the size of a football.[39] Even the largest dinosaurs were very small when first hatched. Remember that the animals that came off the boat were to repopulate the earth. Thus, it would have been necessary to choose young adults, which would soon be in the prime of their reproductive life, to go on the Ark. Recent research suggests that dinosaurs underwent rapid adolescent growth spurts.[40] So it is realistic to assume that God would have sent young adults to the Ark, not fully grown creatures.

Some might argue that the 600 or more named species of dinosaurs could not have fit on the Ark. But Genesis 6:20 states that representative *kinds* of land animals boarded the Ark. The question then is, what is a "kind" (Hebrew: *min*)? Biblical creationists have pointed out that there can be many species descended from a kind. For example, there are many types of cats in the world, but all cat species probably came from only a few kinds of cats originally.[41] The cat varieties today have developed by natural and artificial selection acting on the original variation in the information (genes) of the original cats. This has produced different combinations and subsets of information, and thus different types of cats.

Mutations (errors in copying of the genes during reproduction) can also contribute to the variation, but the changes caused by mutations are "downhill," causing loss of the original information.

Even speciation could occur through these processes. This speciation is *not* "evolution," since it is based on the created information *already present* and is thus a limited, downhill process, not involving an upward increase in complexity. Thus, only a few feline pairs would have been needed on Noah's Ark.

Dinosaur names have tended to proliferate, with new names being given to just a few pieces of bone, even if the skeleton looks similar to one that is a different size or found in a different country. There were probably fewer than 50 distinct groups or kinds of dinosaurs that had to be on the Ark.[42]

Also, it must be remembered that Noah's Ark was extremely large and quite capable of carrying the number of animals needed, including dinosaurs.

The land animals that were not on the Ark, including dinosaurs, drowned. Many were preserved in the layers formed by the Flood—thus the millions of fossils. Presumably, many of the dinosaur fossils were buried at this time, around 4,500 years ago. Also, after the Flood, there would have been considerable catastrophism, including such events as the Ice Age, resulting in some post-Flood formation of fossils, too.

The contorted shapes of these animals preserved in the rocks, the massive numbers of them in fossil graveyards, their wide distribution, and some whole skeletons, all provide convincing evidence that they were buried rapidly, testifying to massive flooding.[43]

Why don't we see dinosaurs today?

At the end of the Flood, Noah, his family, and the animals came out of the Ark (Genesis 8:15–17). The dinosaurs thus began a new life in a new world. Along with the other animals, the dinosaurs came out to breed and repopulate the earth. They would have left the landing place of the Ark and spread over the earth's surface. The descendants of these dinosaurs gave rise to the dragon legends.

But the world they came out to repopulate differed from the one they knew before Noah's Flood. The Flood had devastated it. It was now a much more difficult world in which to survive.

After the Flood, God told Noah that from then on, the animals would fear man, and that animal flesh could be food for man (Genesis 9:1–7). Even for man, the world had become a harsher place. To survive, the once easily obtained plant nutrition would now have to be supplemented by animal sources.

Both animals and man would find their ability to survive tested to the utmost. We can see from the fossil record, from the written history of man, and from experience over recent centuries, that many forms of life on this planet have not survived that test.

We need to remember that many plants and air-breathing, land-dwelling animals have become extinct *since* the Flood— either due to man's action or competition with other species, or because of the harsher post-Flood environment. Many groups are still becoming extinct. Dinosaurs seem to be numbered among the extinct groups.

Why then are people so intrigued about dinosaurs and have little interest in the extinction of the fern *Cladophebius*, for example? It's the dinosaurs' appeal as monsters that excites and fascinates people.

Evolutionists have capitalized on this fascination, and the world is awash with evolutionary propaganda centered on dinosaurs. As a result, evolutionary philosophy has permeated modern thinking, even among Christians.

If you were to ask the zoo why they have endangered species programs, you would probably get an answer something like this: "We've lost lots of animals from this earth. Animals are becoming extinct all the time. Look at all the animals that are gone forever. We need to act to save the animals." If you then asked, "Why are animals becoming extinct?" you might get an answer like this: "It's obvious! People killing them, lack of food, man destroying the environment, diseases, genetic problems, catastrophes like floods—there are lots of reasons."

If you then asked, "Well, what happened to the dinosaurs?" the answer would probably be, "We don't know! Scientists have suggested dozens of possible reasons, but it's a mystery."

Maybe one of the reasons dinosaurs are extinct is that we did not start our endangered species programs early enough. The factors that cause extinction today, which came about because of man's sin—the Curse, the aftermath of the Flood (a judgment), etc.—are the same factors that caused the dinosaurs to become extinct.

Are dinosaurs really extinct?

One cannot prove an organism is extinct without having knowledge of every part of the earth's surface simultaneously. Experts have been embarrassed when, after having declared animals extinct, they were discovered alive and well. For example, in the 1990s explorers found elephants in Nepal that have many features of mammoths.[44]

Scientists in Australia found some living trees that they thought had become extinct with the dinosaurs. One scientist said, "It was like finding a 'live dinosaur.'"[45] When scientists find animals or plants that they thought were extinct long ago, they call them "living fossils." There are hundreds of living fossils, a big embarrassment for those who believe in millions of years of earth history.

Explorers and natives in Africa have reported sighting dinosaur-like creatures, even in the twentieth century.[46] These have usually been confined to out-of-the-way places such as lakes deep in the Congo jungles. Descriptions certainly fit those of dinosaurs.[47]

Cave paintings by native Americans seem to depict a dinosaur.[48] Scientists accept the mammoth drawings in the cave, so why not the dinosaur drawings? Evolutionary indoctrination that man did not live at the same time as dinosaurs stops most scientists from even considering that the drawings are of dinosaurs.

It certainly would be no embarrassment to a creationist if someone discovered a dinosaur living in a jungle. However, this should embarrass evolutionists.

And no, we cannot clone a dinosaur, as in the movie *Jurassic Park*, even if we had dinosaur DNA. We would also need a living female dinosaur. Scientists have found that to clone an animal they need an egg of a living female, since "machinery" in the cytoplasm of her egg is necessary for the new creature to develop.[49]

Birdosaurs?

Many evolutionists do not really think dinosaurs are extinct anyway. In 1997, at the entrance to the bird exhibit at the zoo in Cincinnati, Ohio, we read the following on a sign:

> Dinosaurs went extinct millions of years ago—or did they? No, birds are essentially modern short-tailed feathered dinosaurs.

In the mid-1960s, Dr. John Ostrom from Yale University began to popularize the idea that dinosaurs evolved into birds.[50] However, not all evolutionists agree with this. "It's just a fantasy of theirs," says Alan Feduccia, an ornithologist at the University of North Carolina at Chapel Hill, and a leading critic of the dino-to-bird theory. "They so much want to see living dinosaurs that now they think they can study them vicariously at the backyard bird feeder."[51]

There have been many attempts to indoctrinate the public to believe that modern birds are really dinosaurs. *Time* magazine, on April 26, 1993, had a front page cover of a "birdosaur," now called *Mononykus*, with feathers (a supposed transitional form between dinosaurs and birds) based on a fossil find that had *no* feathers.[52] In the same month, *Science News* had an article suggesting this animal was a digging creature more like a mole.[53]

In 1996, newspapers reported a find in China of a reptile fossil that supposedly had feathers.[54] Some of the media reports claimed that, if it were confirmed, it would be "irrefutable evidence that today's birds evolved from dinosaurs." One scientist stated, "You can't come to any conclusion other than that they're feathers."[55] However, in 1997 the Academy of Natural Sciences in Philadelphia sent four leading scientists to investigate this find. They concluded that they were *not* feathers. The media report stated, concerning one of the scientists, "He said he saw 'hair-like' structures—not hairs—that could have supported a frill, or crest, like those on iguanas."[56]

No sooner had this report appeared than another media report claimed that 20 fragments of bones of a reptile found in South America showed that dinosaurs were related to birds.[57]

Birds are warm-blooded and reptiles are cold-blooded, but evolutionists who believe dinosaurs evolved into birds would like to see dinosaurs as warm-blooded to support their theory. But Dr. Larry Martin, of the University of Kansas, opposes this idea:

> Recent research has shown the microscopic structure of dinosaur bones was "characteristic of cold-blooded animals," Martin said. "So we're back to cold-blooded dinosaurs."[58]

Sadly, the secular media have become so blatant in their anti-Christian stand and pro-evolutionary propaganda that they are bold enough to make such ridiculous statements as, "Parrots and hummingbirds are also dinosaurs."[59]

Several more recent reports have fueled the bird/dinosaur debate among evolutionists. One concerns research on the embryonic origins of the "fingers" of birds and dinosaurs, showing that birds could *not* have evolved from dinosaurs.[60] A study of the so-called feathered dinosaur from China revealed that the dinosaur had a distinctively reptilian lung and diaphragm, which is distinctly different from the avian lung.[61] Another report said that the frayed edges that some thought to be "feathers" on the Chinese fossil are similar to the collagen fibers found immediately beneath the skin of sea snakes.[62]

There is *no* credible evidence that dinosaurs evolved into birds.[63] Dinosaurs have always been dinosaurs and birds have always been birds.

What if a dinosaur fossil *were* found with feathers on it? Would that prove that birds evolved from dinosaurs? No, a duck has a duck bill and webbed feet, as does a platypus, but nobody believes that this proves that platypuses evolved from ducks. The belief that reptiles or dinosarus evolved into birds requires reptilian scales on the way to becoming feathers, that is, transitional scales, not fully formed feathers. A dinosaur-like fossil with feathers would just be another curious mosaic, like the platypus, and part of the pattern of similarities placed in creatures to show the hand of the one true Creator God who made everything.

Why does it matter?

Although dinosaurs are fascinating, some readers may say, "Why are dinosaurs such a big deal? Surely there are many more important issues to deal with in today's world, such as abortion, family breakdown, racism, promiscuity, dishonesty, homosexual behavior, euthanasia, suicide, lawlessness, pornography, and so on. In fact, we should be telling people about the gospel of Jesus Christ, not worrying about side issues like dinosaurs."

Actually, the evolutionary teachings on dinosaurs that pervade society *do* have a great bearing on why many will not listen to the gospel, and thus why social problems abound today. If they don't believe the history in the Bible, why would anyone trust its moral aspects and message of salvation?

If we accept the evolutionary teachings on dinosaurs, then we must accept that the Bible's account of history is false. If the Bible is wrong in this area, then it is not the Word of God and we can ignore everything else it says that we find inconvenient.

If everything made itself through natural processes—without God—then God does not own us and has no right to tell us how to live. In fact, God does not really exist in this way of thinking, so there is no absolute basis for morality. Without God, anything goes—concepts of right and wrong are just a matter of opinion. And without a basis for morality, there is no such thing as sin. And no sin means that there is no need to fear God's judgment and there is no need for the Savior, Jesus Christ. The history in the Bible is vital for properly understanding why one needs to accept Jesus Christ.

Millions of years and the gospel

The teaching that dinosaurs lived and died millions of years before man directly attacks the foundations of the gospel in another way. The fossil record, of which dinosaurs form a part, documents death, disease, suffering, cruelty, and brutality. It is a very ugly record. Allowing for millions of years in the fossil layers means accepting death, bloodshed, disease, and suffering *before* Adam's sin.

But the Bible makes it clear that death, bloodshed, disease, and suffering are a *consequence of sin*. As part of the Curse, God told Adam in Genesis 3:19 that he would return to the dust from which he was made, showing that the sentence of death was not only spiritual, but physical as well.

After Adam disobeyed God, the Lord clothed Adam and Eve with "coats of skins" (Genesis 3:21). To do this He must have killed and shed the blood of at least one animal. The reason for this can be summed up by Hebrews 9:22:

> And according to the law almost all things are purified with blood, and without shedding of blood there is no remission.

God required the shedding of blood for the forgiveness of sins. What happened in the Garden of Eden was a picture of what was to come in Jesus Christ, who shed His blood on the Cross as "the Lamb of God, who takes away the sin of the world" (John 1:29).

If the shedding of blood occurred before sin, as would have happened if the garden was sitting on a fossil record of dead things millions of years old, then the foundation of the Atonement would be destroyed.

This big picture also fits with Romans 8, which says that the whole creation "groans" because of the effects of the Fall of Adam—it was not "groaning" with death and suffering before Adam sinned. Jesus Christ suffered physical death and shed His blood because death was the penalty for sin. Paul discusses this in detail in Romans 5 and 1 Corinthians 15.

Rev 21–22 make it clear that there will be a "new heaven and a new earth" one day where there will be "no more death" and "no more curse"—just as it was before sin changed everything. Obviously, if there are going to be animals in the new earth, they will not die or eat each other or eat the redeemed people.

Thus, the teaching of millions of years of death, disease, and suffering before Adam sinned is a direct attack on the foundation of the message of the Cross.

Conclusion

If we accept God's Word, beginning with Genesis, as being true and authoritative, then we can explain dinosaurs and make sense of the evidence we observe in the world around us. In doing this, we are helping people see that Genesis is absolutely trustwor-thy and logically defensible, and is what it claims to be—the true account of the history of the universe and mankind. And what one believes concerning the book of Genesis will ultimately determine what one believes about the rest of the Bible. This, in turn, will affect how a person views himself or herself, fellow human beings, and what life is all about, including their need for salvation.

1.   J. Horner and D. Lessem, *The Complete T. Rex*, Simon & Schuster, New York, 1993, 18; M. Norell, E. Gaffney and L. Dingus, *Discovering Dinosaurs in the American Museum of Natural History*, Nevraumont Publ., New York, 1995, 17, says that the oldest dinosaur fossil is dated at 228 million years.

2.   D. Gish, *Evolution: the Fossils Still Say No!* Institute for Creation Research, El Cajon, California, 1995, 129ff, discusses evolutionists' views from a creationist position; Norell et al., *Discovering Dinosaurs in the American Museum of Natural History*, 2: "Dinosaurs belong to a group called Archosauria . . . . The living Archosauria are the twenty-one extant crocodiles and alligators, along with the more than ten thousand species of living theropod dinosaurs (birds)."

3.   J. Morris, *The Young Earth*, Master Books, Green Forest, Arkansas, 1994; H. Morris, *The Genesis Record*, Baker Book House, Grand Rapids, Michigan, 1976, 42–46. On the biblical chronology, see J. Ussher, *The Annals of the World*, Master Books, Green Forest, Arkansas, 2003; original published in 1658.

4.   M. Benton, *Dinosaurs: An A–Z Guide*, Derrydale Books, New York, 1988, 10–11.

5.   Benton, *Dinosaurs: An A–Z Guide*. See also D. Lambert and the Diagram Group, *The Dinosaur Data Book*, Avon Books, New York, 1990, 10–35; Norell, et al., *Discovering Dinosaurs in the American Museum of Natural History*, 62–69; V. Sharpton and P. Ward, Eds., *Global Catastrophes in Earth History*, The Geological Society of America, Special Paper 247, 1990.

6.   M. Lemonick, "Parenthood, dino-style," *Time*, p. 48, January 8, 1996.

7.   Psalm 78:5; 2 Timothy 3:14–17; and 2 Peter 1:19–21. God, who inspired the writing, has always existed, is perfect and never lies (Titus 1:2).

8.   D. Lambert, *A Field Guide to Dinosaurs*, Avon Books, New York, 1983, 17.

9.   If some dinosaurs were aquatic, then these would have been created on Day 5 of Creation Week.

10.   S. West, "Dinosaur head hunt," *Science News* 116(18):314–315, 1979. Originally assem-bled wrongly with the head of a Camarasaurus-type dinosaur on an Apatosaurus skeleton and later corrected with the right head, which was from "the same family as its nearly identical cousin, Diplodocus," p. 314.

11.   Benton, *Dinosaurs: An A-Z Guide*, 14.

12.   Lambert et al., *The Dinosaur Data Book*, 279.

13.   Morris, *The Young Earth*, 51–67.

14.   Morris, *The Genesis Record*, 44–46.

15.   J. Stambaugh, "Creation, suffering and the problem of evil," *CEN Technical Journal* 10(3):391–404, 1996.

16. The KJV most often used today is actually the 1769 revision by Benjamin Blayney of Oxford.

17. D. Dixon et al., *The Macmillan Illustrated Encyclopedia of Dinosaurs and Prehistoric Animals*, Macmillan Publishing Co., New York, 1998, 92; R. Grigg, "Dinosaurs and dragons: stamping on the legends!" *Creation*, 14(3):11, 1990.

18. D. Norman, *The Illustrated Encyclopedia of Dinosaurs*, Salamander Books Limited, London, 1985, 8. The meaning of "terrible lizard" has helped popularize the idea that dinosaurs were all gigantic savage monsters. This is far from the truth. Had Owen known about the *smaller* dinosaurs, he may never have coined the word.

19. The Hebrew words have a range of meanings, including "sea monster" (Gen. 1:21; Job 7:12; Psa. 148:7; Isa. 27:1; Ezek. 29:3, 32:2) and "serpent" (Exod. 7:9; cf. Exod. 4:3 and Hebrew parallelism of Deut. 32:33). *Tannin/m* are fearsome creatures, inhabiting remote, desolate places (Isa. 34:13, 35:7; Jer. 49:33, 51:37; Mal. 1:8), difficult to kill (Isa. 27:1, 51:9) and/or serpentine (Deut. 32:33; cf. Psa. 91:13) and/or having feet (Ezek. 32:2). However, *tannin* are referred to as suckling their young (Lam. 4:3), which is not a feature of reptiles, but of whales (sea monsters?), for example. The word(s) seems to refer to large, fearsome creatures that dwelled in swampy areas or in the water. The term could include reptiles and mammals. Modern translators often render the words as "jackals," but this seems inappropriate because jackals are not particularly fearsome or difficult to kill and don't live in swamps.

20. S. Czerkas and S. Czerkas, *Dinosaurs: A Global View*, Barnes and Noble Books, Spain, 1996, 179; P. Booker, "A new candidate for Leviathan?" *TJ* 19(2):14–16, 2005.

21. D. Norman, *The Illustrated Encyclopedia of Dinosaurs*, Gramercy, New York, 1988, 170–172; P. Wellnhofer, *Pterosaurs: The Illustrated Encyclopedia of Prehistoric Flying Reptiles*, Barnes and Noble, New York, 1991, 83–85, 135–136.

22. E.g., *NIV Study Bible*, Zondervan, Grand Rapids, Michigan, 1985.

23. New Living Translation: Holy Bible, Tyndale House Publishers, Wheaton, Illinois, 1996. Job 40:15: "Take a look at the mighty hippopotamus."

24. P. Taylor, *The Great Dinosaur Mystery*, Films for Christ, Mesa, Arizona, 1991. See also P. Taylor, *The Great Dinosaur Mystery and the Bible*, Accent Publications, Denver, Colorado, 1989.

25. D. Swift, "Messages on stone," *Creation* 19(2):20–23, 1997.

26. C. Wieland, "Sensational dinosaur blood report," *Creation* 19(4):42–43, 1997.

27. D. Batten, "Buddy Davis—the creation music man (who makes dinosaurs)," *Creation* 19(3):49–51, 1997; M. Helder, "Fresh dinosaur bones found," *Creation* 14(3):16–17, 1992.

28. M. Schweitzer and T. Staedter, "The real Jurassic Park," *Earth*, pp. 55–57, June 1997. See report in *Creation* 19(4):42–43, which describes the careful testing that showed that hemoglobin was present.

29. K. Davies, "Duckbill dinosaurs (Hadrosauridae, Ornithischia) from the North Slope of Alaska," *Journal of Paleontology* 61(1):198–200, 1987.

30. Batten, "Buddy Davis—the creation music man," 1997.

31. S. Lucas, *Dinosaurs: The Textbook*, Wm. C. Brown Publishers, Dubuque, IA, 1994, 194–196.

32. D. Marrs and V. Kylberg, *Dino Cardz*, 1991. *Estemmenosuchus* was a large mammal-like reptile. "Despite having menacing-looking fangs it apparently was a plant-eater." The authors possibly concluded this from its rear teeth.

33. K. Brandes, *Vanishing Species*, Time-Life Books, New York, 1974, 98.

34. P. Weston, "Bats: sophistication in miniature," *Creation* 21(1):28–31, 1999.

35. Morris, *The Genesis Record*, 78.

36. See chapter 21 of *The New Answers Book 1* for more on the possible origin of defense-attack structures.

37. For example, D. Ager, *The New Catastrophism*, Cambridge University Press, Cambridge, UK, 1993.

38. M. Crichton, *The Lost World*, Ballantine Books, New York, 1995, 122. "Dinosaurs were mostly small . . . . People always think they were huge, but the average dinosaur was the size of a sheep or a small pony." According to Horner and Lessem, *The Complete T. Rex*, 1993, 124: "Most dinosaurs were smaller than bulls."

39. D. Lambert, *A Field Guide to Dinosaurs*, Avon Books, New York, 1983, 127.

40. G.M. Erickson, K.C. Rogers, and S.A. Yerby, "Dinosaurian growth patterns and rapid avian growth rates," *Nature* 412(6845):405–408, 429–433, July 26, 2001.

41. W. Mehlert, "On the origin of cats and carnivores," *CEN Technical Journal*, 9(1):106–120, 1995.

42. Norell et al., *Discovering Dinosaurs in the American Museum of Natural History*, figure 56, pp. 86–87. See Czerkas and Czerkas, *Dinosaurs: A Global View*, 151.

43. For example, reptiles drowned in a flash flood 200 million years ago, according to the interpretation put upon the reptile fossils discovered in Lubbock Quarry, Texas (*The Weekend Australian*, p. 32, November 26–27, 1983).

44. C. Wieland, "'Lost World' animals found!" *Creation* 19(1):10–13, 1996.

45. Anon., "Sensational Australian tree ... like 'finding a live dinosaur,'" *Creation* 17(2):13, 1995. See Anon., *Melbourne Sun*, February 6, 1980. More than 40 people claimed to have seen *plesiosaurs* off the Victorian coast (Australia) over recent years.

46. Anon., "Dinosaur hunt," *Science Digest* 89(5):21, 1981. See H. Regusters, "Mokele-mbembe: an investigation into rumors concerning a strange animal in the Republic of Congo, 1981," *Munger Africana Library Notes*, 64: 2–32, 1982; M. Agmagna, "Results of the first Congolese mokele-mbembe expedition," *Cryptozoology* 2:103, 1983, as cited in *Science Frontiers 33*, 1983.

47. D. Catchpoole, "Mokele-mbembe: a living dinosaur?" *Creation* 21(4):24–25, 1999.

48. D. Swift, "Messages on stone," *Creation*, 19(2):20–23, 1997.

49. C. Wieland, "Hello Dolly!" *Creation* 19(3):23, 1997.

50. Norell, *Discovering Dinosaurs in the American Museum of Natural History*, 13.

51. V. Morell, "Origin of birds: the dinosaur debate," *Audubon*, March– April 1997, p. 38.

52. Anon., "New 'birdosaur' not missing link!" *Creation* 15(3):3, 1993.

53. Anon., "'Birdosaur' more like a mole," *Creation* 15(4):7, 1993.

54. M. Browne, "Downy dinosaur reported," *Cincinnati Enquirer*, p. A13, October 19, 1996.

55. Anon., "Remains of feathered dinosaur bolster theory on origin of birds," Associated Press, New York, October 18, 1996.

56. B. Stieg, "Bones of contention," *Philadelphia Inquirer*, March 31, 1997.

57. P. Recer, "Birds linked to dinosaurs," *Cincinnati Enquirer*, p. A9, May 21, 1997.

58. Stieg, "Did birds evolve from dinosaurs?" *The Philadelphia Inquirer*, March 1997.

59. P. Recer, "Birds linked to dinosaurs," 1997.

60. A. Burke and A. Feduccia, "Developmental patterns and the identification of homologies in the avian hand," *Science* 278:666–668, 1997; A. Feduccia and J. Nowicki, "The hand of birds revealed by early bird embryos," *Naturwissenschaften* 89:391–393, 2002.

61. J. Ruben et al., "Lung structure and ventilation in theropod dinosaurs and early birds," *Science* 278:1267–1270, 1997.

62. A. Gibbons, "Plucking the feathered dinosaur," *Science* 278:1229, 1997.

63. For more on the problems with dinosaur-to-bird evolution, see the next chapter in this book.

Ken Ham is President and CEO of Answers in Genesis–USA and the Creation Museum. Ken's bachelor's degree in applied science (with an emphasis on environmental biology) was awarded by the Queensland Institute of Technology in Australia. He also holds a diploma of education from the University of Queensland. In recognition of the contribution Ken has made to the church in the USA and internationally, Ken has been awarded two honorary doctorates: a Doctor of Divinity (1997) from Temple Baptist College in Cincinnati, Ohio and a Doctor of Literature (2004) from Liberty University in Lynchburg, Virginia.

Ken has authored or coauthored many books concerning the authority and accuracy of God's Word and the effects of evolutionary thinking, including *Genesis of a Legacy* and *The Lie: Evolution*.

Since moving to America in 1987, Ken has become one of the most in-demand Christian conference speakers and talk show guests in America. He has appeared on national shows such as Fox's *The O'Reilly Factor* and *Fox and Friends in the Morning*; CNN's *The Situation Room with Wolf Blitzer*, ABC's *Good Morning America*, the BBC, *CBS News Sunday Morning*, *The NBC Nightly News with Brian Williams*, and *The PBS News Hour with Jim Lehrer*.

Did Dinosaurs Turn into Birds?

by David Menton

According to many evolutionists today, dinosaurs are really not extinct but rather are feeding at our bird feeders even as we speak. For many evolutionists, it would seem, birds simply *are* dinosaurs. With this sort of bias, it is quite easy for evolutionists to find supposed evidence to support the notion that birds evolved from dinosaurs.

But what does the Bible tell us about the origin of birds, and just how good is the scientific evidence that some dinosaurs evolved into birds?

What does the Bible say about the origin of birds?

Birds were created on day 5 and dinosaurs on day 6

In the first chapter of Genesis, verse 21, we read that on Day 5 of creation, God created "every winged fowl after its kind." This includes birds that flew above the earth (Genesis 1:20). Man and land animals were created on Day 6 of the Creation Week (Genesis 1:24–31). Were there land birds that didn't fly originally? I would leave open the possibility, but a discussion of this is beyond the scope of this chapter. Most ornithologists say that these birds are *secondarily* flightless (i.e., they lost the ability to fly). This would be due to variance within kind or to mutational losses since creation. So, the best possibility is that birds were created on Day 5 as flyers, and some have lost this ability, but I wouldn't be dogmatic.

The extinct aquatic reptiles, such as the plesiosaurs, and the extinct flying reptiles, such as the pterodactyls, are not classified as dinosaurs, and most evolutionists do not believe that they evolved into birds. Thus, for the Bible-believing Christian, both the fact of creation and the order of creation affirm that birds and dinosaurs originated separately.

Birds are of many different "kinds"

Genesis 1:21 says that God created every winged bird after its "kind." The following verse says they were to multiply, or reproduce; so the logical connection is that birds of the same kind can reproduce. The Hebrew word for "kind" in Genesis refers to any group of animals capable of interbreeding and reproducing according to their type. For example, all dogs and dog-like animals, such as wolves and coyotes, are capable of interbreeding and thus would represent one "kind," even though some are classified today as different species.

This does not mean, however, that all birds represent a single created kind and thus share a common ancestry. The Bible tells us that there are many different bird kinds (plural). The Levitical dietary laws (Leviticus 11:13–19), for example, list many different bird kinds as being unclean. This gives further biblical support for multiple created bird kinds.

What do evolutionists claim about the origin of birds?

Evolutionists have long speculated that birds evolved from reptiles. At one time or another, virtually every living and extinct class of reptiles has been proposed as the ancestor of birds. The famous Darwinian apologist Thomas Huxley was the first to speculate (in the mid 1800s) that birds evolved from dinosaurs.

While this notion has gone in and out of favor over the years, it is currently a popular view among evolutionists. Indeed, the origin of birds from dinosaurs is touted as irrefutable dogma in our schools, biology textbooks, and the popular media.

While evolutionists now agree that birds are related in some way to dinosaurs, they are divided over whether birds evolved from some early shared ancestor of the dinosaurs within the archosauria (which includes alligators, pterosaurs, plesiosaurs, ichthyosaurs, and thecodonts) or directly from advanced theropod dinosaurs (bipedal meat-eating dinosaurs, such as the wellknown *Tyrannosaurus rex*). The latter view has gained in popularity since 1970, when John Ostrom discovered a rather "bird-like" early Cretaceous theropod dinosaur called *Deinonychus*.

An adult *Deinonychus* measured about 12 feet (3.5 m) long, weighed over 150 pounds (68 kg), and was about 5 feet (1.5 m) tall standing on its two hind legs. Like other theropods (which means "beast foot"), *Deinonychus* had forelimbs much smaller than its hind limbs, with hands bearing three fingers and feet bearing three toes. The most distinctive feature of *Deinonychus* (which means "terrible claw") is a large curved talon on its middle toe.

One of the main reasons that *Deinonychus* and other similar theropod dinosaurs (called dromaeosaurs) seemed to be plausible ancestors to birds is that, like birds, these creatures walked solely on their hind legs and have only three digits on their hands. But as we shall see, there are many problems with transforming any dinosaur, and particularly a theropod, into a bird.

Problems with dinosaurs evolving into birds

Warm-blooded vs. cold-blooded

Seemingly forgotten in all the claims that birds are essentially dinosaurs (or at least that they evolved from dinosaurs) is the fact that dinosaurs are reptiles. There are many differences between birds and reptiles, including the fact that (with precious few exceptions) living reptiles are cold-blooded creatures, while birds and mammals are warm-blooded. Indeed, even compared to most mammals, birds have exceptionally *high* body temperatures resulting from a high metabolic rate.

The difference between cold- and warm-blooded animals isn't simply in the relative temperature of the blood but rather in their ability to maintain a constant body core temperature. Thus, warm-blooded animals such as birds and mammals have internal physiological mechanisms to maintain an essentially constant body temperature; they are more properly called "endothermic." In contrast, reptiles have a varying body temperature influenced by their surrounding environment and are called "ectothermic." An ectothermic animal can adjust its body temperature behaviorally (e.g., moving between shade and sun), even achieving higher body temperature than a so-called warm-blooded animal, but this is done by outside factors.

In an effort to make the evolution of dinosaurs into birds seem more plausible, some evolutionists have argued that dinosaurs were also endothermic,[1] but there is no clear evidence for this.[2]

One of the lines of evidence for endothermic dinosaurs is based on the microscopic structure of dinosaur bones. Fossil dinosaur bones have been found containing special microscopic structures called osteons (or Haversian systems). Osteons are complex concentric layers of bone surrounding blood vessels in areas where the bone is dense. This arrangement is assumed by some to be unique to endothermic animals and thus evidence that dinosaurs are endothermic, but such is not the case. Larger vertebrates (whether reptiles, birds, or mammals) may also have this type of bone. Even tuna fish have osteonal bone in their vertebral arches.

Another argument for endothermy in dinosaurs is based on the eggs and assumed brood behavior of dinosaurs, but this speculation too has been challenged.[3] There is in fact no theropod brooding behavior not known to occur in crocodiles and other cold-blooded living reptiles.

Alan Feduccia, an expert on birds and their evolution, has concluded that "there has never been, nor is there now, any evidence that dinosaurs were endothermic."[4] Feduccia says that despite the lack of evidence "many authors have tried to make specimens conform to the hot-blooded theropod dogma."

"Bird-hipped" vs. "lizard-hipped" dinosaurs

All dinosaurs are divided into two major groups based on the structure of their hips (pelvic bones): the lizard-hipped dinosaurs (saurischians) and the bird-hipped dinosaurs (ornithiscians). The main difference between the two hip structures is that the pubic bone of the bird-hipped dinosaurs is directed toward the rear (as it is in birds) rather than entirely to the front (as it is in mammals and reptiles).

But in most other respects, the bird-hipped dinosaurs, including such huge quadrupedal sauropods as *Brachiosaurus* and *Diplodocus*, are even less bird-like than the lizard-hipped, bipedal dinosaurs such as the theropods. This point is rarely emphasized in popular accounts of dinosaur/bird evolution.

The three-fingered hand

One of the main lines of evidence cited by evolutionists for the evolution of birds from theropod dinosaurs is the three-fingered "hand" found in both birds and theropods. The problem is that recent studies have shown that there is a digital mismatch between birds and theropods.

Most terrestrial vertebrates have an embryological development based on the five-fingered hand. In the case of birds and theropod dinosaurs, two of the five fingers are lost (or greatly reduced) and three are retained during development of the embryo. If birds evolved from theropods, one would expect the same three fingers to be retained in both birds and theropod dinosaurs, but such is not the case. Evidence shows that the fingers retained in theropod dinosaurs are fingers 1, 2, and 3 (the "thumb" is finger 1) while the fingers retained in birds are 2, 3, and 4.[5]

Avian vs. reptilian lung

One of the most distinctive features of birds is their lungs. Bird lungs are small in size and nearly rigid, but they are, nevertheless, highly efficient to meet the high metabolic needs of flight. Bird respiration involves a unique "flow-through ventilation" into a set of nine interconnecting flexible air sacs sandwiched between muscles and under the skin. The air sacs contain few blood vessels and do not take part in oxygen exchange, but rather function like bellows to move air through the lungs.

The air sacs permit a unidirectional flow of air through the lungs resulting in higher oxygen content than is possible with the bidirectional air flow through the lungs of reptiles and mam-

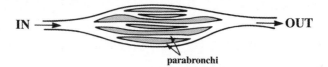

parabronchi

mals. The air flow moves through the same tubes at different times both into and out of the lungs of reptiles and mammals, and this results in a mixture of oxygen-rich air with oxygen-depleted air (air that has been in the lungs for awhile). The unidirectional flow through bird lungs not only permits more oxygen to diffuse into the blood but also keeps the volume of air in the lungs nearly constant, a requirement for maintaining a level flight path.

bronchi

alveoli

If theropod dinosaurs are the ancestors of birds, one might expect to find evidence of an avian-type lung in such dinosaurs. While fossils generally do not preserve soft tissue such as lungs, a very fine theropod dinosaur fossil (*Sinosauropteryx*) has been found in which the outline of the visceral cavity has been well preserved. The evidence clearly indicates that this theropod had lung and respiratory mechanics similar to that of a crocodile—not a bird.[6] Specifically, there was evidence of a diaphragm-like muscle separating the lung from the liver, much as you see in modern crocodiles (birds lack a diaphragm). These observations suggest that this theropod was similar to an ectothermic reptile, not an endothermic bird.

Origin of feathers

Do feathered dinosaurs exist?

Feathers have long been considered to be unique to birds. Certainly all living birds have feathers of some kind, while no living creature other than birds has been found to have a cutaneous appendage even remotely similar to a feather. Since most evolutionists are certain that birds evolved from dinosaurs (or at least are closely related to them), there has been an intense effort to find dinosaur fossils that show some suggestion of feathers or "protofeathers." With such observer bias, one must be skeptical of recent widely publicized reports of feathered dinosaurs.

Dinosaurs are reptiles, and so it is not surprising that fossil evidence has shown them to have a scaly skin typical of reptiles. For example, a recently discovered well-preserved specimen of *Compsognathus* (a small theropod dinosaur of the type believed to be most closely related to birds) showed unmistakable evidence of scales but alas—no feathers.[7]

Still, there have been many claims of feathered dinosaurs, particularly from fossils found in Liaoning province in northeastern China.[8] The earliest feathered dinosaur from this source is the very unbird-like dinosaur *Sinosauropteryx*, which lacks any evidence of structures that could be shown to be feather-like.[9]

Structures described as "protofeathers" in the dinosaur fossils *Sinosauropteryx* and *Sinithosaurus* are filamentous and sometimes have interlaced structures bearing no obvious resemblance to feathers. It now appears likely that these filaments (often referred to as "dino-fuzz") are actually connective tissue fibers (collagen) found in the deep dermal layer of the skin. Feduccia laments that "the major and most worrying problem of the feathered dinosaur hypothesis is that the integumental structures have been homologized with avian feathers on the basis of anatomically and paleontologically unsound and misleading information."[10]

Complicating matters even further is the fact that true birds have been found among the Liaoning province fossils in the same layers as their presumed dinosaur ancestors. The obvious bird fossil *Confuciusornis sanctus*, for example, has long slender tail feathers resembling those of a modern scissor-tail flycatcher. Two taxa (*Caudipteryx* and *Protarchaeopteryx*) that were thought to be dinosaurs with true feathers are now generally conceded to be flightless birds.[11]

Thus far, the only obvious dinosaur fossil with obvious feathers that was "found" is *Archaeoraptor liaoningensis*. This so-called definitive feathered dinosaur was reported with much fanfare in the November 1999 issue of *National Geographic* but has since been shown to be a fraud.

What would it prove if features common to one type of animal were found on another? Nothing. Simply put, God uses various designs with various creatures. Take the platypus, for example—a mosaic. It has several design features that are shared with other animals, and yet it is completely distinct. So if a dinosaur (or mammal) is ever found with feathers, it would call into question our human criteria for classification, not biblical veracity. What's needed to support evolution is *not* an unusual mosaic of complete traits, but a trait in transition, such as a "scale-feather," what creationist biologists would call a "sceather."

Feathers and scales are dissimilar

If birds evolved from dinosaurs or any other reptile, then feathers must have evolved from reptilian scales. Evolutionists are so confident that feathers evolved from scales that they often claim that feathers are very similar to scales. The popular Encarta computerized encyclopedia (1997) describes feathers as a "horny outgrowth of skin peculiar to the bird but similar in structure and origin to the scales of fish and reptiles."[12]

In actual fact, feathers are profoundly different from scales in both their structure and growth. Feathers grow individually from tube-like follicles similar to hair follicles. Reptilian scales, on the other hand, are not individual follicular structures but rather comprise a continuous sheet on the surface of the body. Thus, while feathers grow and are shed individually (actually in symmetrically matched pairs!), scales grow and are shed as an entire sheet of skin.

The feather vane is made up of hundreds of barbs, each bearing hundreds of barbules interlocked with tiny hinged hooklets.

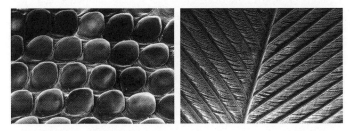

This incredibly complex structure bears not the slightest resemblance to the relatively simple reptilian scale. Still, evolutionists continue to publish imaginative scenarios of how long-fringed reptile scales evolved by chance into feathers, but evidence of "sceathers" eludes them.

Archaeopteryx, a true bird, is older than the "feathered" dinosaurs

One of the biggest dilemmas for those who want to believe that dinosaurs evolved into birds is that the so-called feathered dinosaurs found thus far are dated to be about 20 million years more recent than *Archaeopteryx*. This is a problem for evolution because *Archaeopteryx* is now generally recognized to be a true bird.[13] Some specimens of this bird are so perfectly fossilized that even the microscopic detail of its feathers is clearly visible. So, having alleged missing links of dinosaurs changing into birds when birds already exist doesn't help the case for evolution.

For many years *Archaeopteryx* has been touted in biology text-books and museums as the perfect transitional fossil, presumably being precisely intermediate between reptiles and birds. Much has been made over the fact that *Archaeopteryx* had teeth, fingers on its wings, and a long tail—all supposedly proving its reptilian ancestry. While there are no living birds with teeth, other fossilized birds such as *Hesperornis* also had teeth. Some modern birds, such as the ostrich, have fingers on their wings, and the juvenile hoatzin (a South American bird) has well-developed fingers and toes with which it can climb trees.

Origin of flight

One of the biggest problems for evolutionists is explaining the origin of flight. To make matters worse, evolutionists believe that the flying birds evolved before the nonflying birds, such as penguins.

The theropod type of dinosaur that is believed to have evolved into flying birds is, to say the least, poorly designed for flight. These dinosaurs have small forelimbs that typically can't even reach their mouths. It is not clear what theropods, such as the well-known *T. rex*, did with their tiny front limbs. It is obvious that they didn't walk, feed, or grasp prey with them, and they surely didn't fly with them!

Another problem is that this bipedal type of dinosaur had a long heavy tail to balance the weight of a long neck and large head. Decorating such a creature with feathers would hardly suffice to get it off the ground or be of much benefit in any other way.

Conclusion

Having a true bird appear before alleged feathered dinosaurs, no mechanism to change scales into feathers, no mechanism to change a reptilian lung into an avian lung, and no legitimate dinosaurs found with feathers are all good indications that dinosaurs didn't turn into birds. The evidence is consistent with what the Bible teaches about birds being unique and created after their kinds.

Genesis is clear that God didn't make birds from pre-existing dinosaurs. In fact, dinosaurs (land animals made on Day 6) came *after* winged creatures made on Day 5, according to the Bible. Both biblically and scientifically, chicken eaters around the world can rest easy—they aren't eating mutant dinosaurs.

1. R.T. Bakker, "Dinosaur renaissance," *Scientific American* 232:58–78, 1975.

2. A. Feduccia, "Dinosaurs as reptiles," *Evolution* 27:166–169,1973; A. Feduccia, *The Origin and Evolution of Birds*, 2nd Ed., Yale University Press, New Haven, Connecticut, 1999.

3. N.R. Geist and T.D. Jones, "Juvenile skeletal structure and the reproduction habits of dinosaurs," *Science* 272:712–714,1996.

4. A. Feduccia, T. Lingham-Soliar, and J.R. Hinchliffe, "Do feathered dinosaurs exist? Testing the hypothesis on neontological and paleontological evidence," *Journal of Morphology* 266:125–166, 2005.

5. Feduccia et al., 2005.

6. J.A. Ruben, T.D. Jones, N.R. Geist, and W.J. Hillenius, "Lung structure and ventilation in theropod dinosaurs and early birds," *Science* 278:1267–1270, 1997.

7. U.B. Gohlich and L.M. Chiappe, "A new carnivorous dinosaur from the late Jurassic Solnhofen archipelago," *Nature* 440:329–332, 2006.

8. P.J. Chen, Z.M. Dong, and S.N. Zheng, "An exceptionally well-preserved theropod dinosaur from the Yixian formation of China," *Nature* 391:147–152,1998; X. Xu, X.Wang, and X. Wu, "A dromaeosaurid dinosaur with a filamentous integument from the Yixian formation of China," *Nature* 401:262–266, 1999; P.J. Currie and P.J. Chen, "Anatomy of *Sinosauropteryx prima* from Liaoning, northeastern China," *Can. J. Earth Sci.* 38:1705–1727, 2001.

9. Feduccia et al., 2005.

10. Feduccia et al., 2005.

11. Feduccia et al., 2005.

12. Encarta 98 Encyclopedia. 1993–1997.

13. P.J. Currie et al., eds., *Feathered Dragons: Studies on the Transition from Dinosaurs to Birds*, Indiana University Press, Bloomington, Indiana, 2004.

David Menton received his PhD in Cell Biology from Brown University. Now retired, Dr. Menton served as a biomedical research technician at Mayo Clinic and then as an associate professor of anatomy at Washington University School of Medicine (St. Louis) for more than 30 years. He was a consulting editor in histology for Stedman's Medical Dictionary and has received numerous awards for his teaching. Dr. Menton is a popular speaker for Answers in Genesis, and he presents eye-opening science workshops regularly at the Creation Museum.

Why Don't We Find Human and Dinosaur Fossils Together?

by Bodie Hodge

Biblical creationists believe that man and dinosaurs lived at the same time because God, a perfect eyewitness to history, said that He created man and land animals on Day 6 (Genesis 1:24–31). Dinosaurs are land animals, so logically they were created on Day 6.

In contrast, those who do not believe the plain reading of Genesis, such as many non-Christians and compromising Christians, believe the rock and fossil layers on earth represent millions of years of earth history and that man and dinosaurs did not live at the same time.

Old-earth proponents often argue that if man and dinosaurs lived at the same time, their fossils should be found in the same layers. Since no one has found definitive evidence of human remains in the same layers as dinosaurs (Cretaceous, Jurassic, and Triassic), they say that humans and dinosaurs are separated by millions of years of time and, therefore, didn't live together. So, old-earth proponents ask a very good question: Why don't we find human fossils with dinosaur fossils, if they lived at the same time?

We find human fossils in layers that most creationists consider post-Flood. Most of these were probably buried after the Flood and after the scattering of humans from Babel. So it is true that human and dinosaur fossils have yet to be found in the same layers, but does that mean that long-age believers are correct?

What do we find in the fossil record?

The first issue to consider is what we actually find in the fossil record.

- ~95% of all fossils are shallow marine organisms, such as corals and shellfish.

- ~95% of the remaining 5% are algae and plants.

- ~95% of the remaining 0.25% are invertebrates, including insects.

- The remaining 0.0125% are vertebrates, mostly fish. (95% of land vertebrates consist of less than one bone, and 95% of mammal fossils are from the Ice Age after the Flood.)[1]

The number of dinosaur fossils is actually relatively small, compared to other types of creatures. Since the Flood was a marine catastrophe, we would expect marine fossils to be dominant in the fossil record. And that is the case.

Vertebrates are not as common as other types of life-forms. This makes sense of these percentages and helps us understand why vertebrates, including dinosaurs, are so rare and even overwhelmed by marine organisms in the record.

Yet that still does not explain why there are no fossilized humans in Flood sediments.

Were pre-Flood humans completely obliterated?

In Genesis 6:7 and Genesis 7:23 God says He will "blot out" man from the face of the earth using the Flood. Some have suggested that this phrase means to completely obliterate all evidence of man. However, this is not completely accurate. After a lengthy study, Fouts and Wise make it clear that the Hebrew word hxm (*mahâ*), translated as "blot out" or "destroy," can still leave evidence behind. They say,

Although mahâ is properly translated "blot out," "wipe," or even "destroy," it is not to be understood to refer to the complete obliteration of something without evidence remaining. In every Biblical use of mahâ where it is possible to determine the fate of the blotted, wiped, or destroyed, the continued existence of something is terminated, but evidence may indeed remain of the previous existence and/or the blotting event itself. Even the theological consideration of the "blotting out" of sin suggests that evidence usually remains (e.g., consequences, scars, sin nature, etc.).[2]

In light of this, it is possible that human fossils from the Flood could still exist but just haven't been found yet.

So, should we find human fossils in layers that contain dinosaur fossils? To answer this further, we need to understand what we actually find in the fossil record, what the likelihood is that humans would have been fossilized, what is unusual about their distribution, and how much Flood sediment there was.

Do humans fossilize like other creatures?

Fossilization is a rare event, especially of humans who are very mobile. Since the rains of Noah's Flood took weeks to cover the earth, many people could have made it to boats, grabbed on to floating debris, and so on. Some may have made it to higher ground. Although they wouldn't have lasted that long and would have eventually perished, they might not fossilize.

In most cases, dead things decompose or get eaten. They just disappear and nothing is left. The 2004 tsunami in Southeast Asia was a shocking reminder of the speed with which water and other forces can eliminate all trace of bodies, even when we know where to look. According to the United Nation's Office of the Special Envoy for Tsunami Recovery, nearly 43,000 tsunami victims were never found.[3]

Even if rare, it would still be possible to fossilize a human body. In fact, we do find fossils of humans, such as Neanderthals, in the post-Flood sediments. So why don't we find humans in pre-Flood sediments?

One suggestion has been that the human population was relatively small. Let's see how that possibility bears out.

Were pre-Flood humans few in number?

Estimates for the pre-Flood population are based on very little information, since Genesis 1 doesn't give extensive family size or population growth information. We know that Noah was in the tenth generation of his line, and he lived about 1,650 years after creation. Genesis also indicates that in Noah's lineage children were being born to fathers between the ages of 65 and more than 500 (when Noah bore his three sons).

How many generations were there in other lineages? We don't know. We know that those in the line from Adam to Noah were living upwards of 900 years each, but we can't be certain everyone lived that long. How many total children were born? Again, we don't know. What were the death rates? We simply don't know.

Despite this lack of information, estimates have ranged from a few hundred thousand to 17 billion people.[4] These estimates are based on various population growth rates and numbers of generations. Recall that Noah was in the tenth generation from Adam, however, so these estimates may be too high.

It seems doubtful that there were many hundreds of millions of people before the Flood. If the world was indeed bad enough for God to judge with a Flood, then people were probably blatantly disobedient to God's command to be fruitful and fill the earth. Moreover, the Bible says that violence filled the earth, so death rates may have been extraordinarily high.

In light of this, the population of humans in the pre-Flood world could have been as low as hundreds of thousands. Even if we make a generous assumption of 200 million people at the time of the Flood, there would be just over one human fossil per cubic mile of sediment laid down by the Flood!

Were humans concentrated in high-density pockets that have not been discovered?

Today, humans tend to clump together in groups in towns, villages, and cities. In the same way, people were probably not evenly distributed before the Flood. The first city is recorded in Genesis 4:17, long before the Flood. We know that most of the population today lives within 100 miles (160 km) of the coastline. One report states, "Already nearly two-thirds of humanity—some 3.6 billion people—crowd along a coastline, or live within 150 kilometers of one."[5]

This is strong evidence that the pre-Flood civilizations probably were not evenly distributed on the landmass. If man wasn't evenly distributed, then the pockets of human habitation possibly were buried in places that have not yet been discovered.

Not only is fossilization a rare event, but fossils are also difficult to find. Just consider how much sediment was laid down by the Flood, compared to the area that has actually been exposed for us to explore.

John Woodmorappe's studies indicate that there are about 168 million cubic miles (700 km³) of Flood sediment.[6] John Morris estimates that there is about 350 million cubic miles of Flood sediment.[7] The latter may be high because the total volume of water on the earth is estimated at about 332.5 million cubic miles, according to the U.S. Geological Survey.[8] But even so, there is a lot of sediment left to sift through. Having such a massive amount of sediment to study is a major reason why we have not found human fossils yet.

So, a small human population and massive amounts of sediment are two prominent factors why we haven't found human fossils in pre-Flood sediments. It also may simply be that we haven't found the sediment where humans were living and were buried.

Think about it—would you want to live with dinosaurs?

Often, people believe that if human bones aren't found with dinosaur bones, then they didn't live at the same time. Actually, all we know for sure is that they weren't buried together. It is very easy for creatures to live at the same time on earth, but never even cross paths. Have you ever seen a tiger or a panda in the wild? Just because animals are not found together does not mean they do not live in the same world at the same time.

A great example is the coelacanth. Coelacanth fossils are found in marine deposits below dinosaurs and in other marine layers that date about the same age as dinosaurs.[9] It was once thought the coelacanth became extinct about 70 million years ago because their fossils are not found in any deposits higher than this. However, in 1938 living populations were found in the Indian Ocean.[10] It appears that coelacanths were buried with other sea creatures during the Flood— as we would expect. The example of the coelacanth shows that animals are not necessarily buried in the same place as other animals from different environments. We don't find human bones buried with coelacanths, either, but we live together today, and people are enjoying them for dinner in some parts of the world.

Coelacanths aren't the only example. We find many examples like this, even with creatures that did not live in the sea. One popular example is the Wollemi Pine, which was fossilized in Jurassic deposits, supposedly 150 million years ago.[11] However, we find these trees living today. Another great living fossil is the Ginkgo tree, which supposedly thrived 240 million years ago, prior to the dinosaurs.[12] Yet, they are not found in layers with dinosaurs or post-Flood humans, even though they exist today. The list of "living fossils" goes on. Because animals and plants aren't buried together, it is no indication that things didn't live together.

In fact, based on human nature, we can assume that humans probably chose not to live in the same place with dinosaurs. So, the real issue is what happened to the local environment where humans lived.

What can we conclude?

If human and dinosaur bones are ever found in the same layers, it would be a fascinating find to both creationists and evolutionists. Those who hold a biblical view of history wouldn't be surprised but would consider several logical possibilities, such as human parties invading dinosaur lands for sport or for food, or merely humans and dinosaurs being washed up and buried together.

Evolutionists, on the other hand, who believe the geologic layers represent millions of years of time, would have a real challenge. In the old-earth view, man isn't supposed to be the same age as dinosaurs. Yet we can be sure that this finding would not overturn their starting assumptions—they would simply try to develop a hypothesis consistent with their preconceived view of history. For example, they might search for the possibility that the fossils were moved and redeposited.

So, ultimately, the debate is not about the evidence itself—where we find human fossils and dinosaur fossils. Nobody was there to actually observe humans and dinosaurs living together. We are forced to reconstruct that history based on our existing assumptions about time and history, as well as our limited fossil evidence from the rocks.

As biblical creationists, we don't require that human and dinosaur fossils be found in the same layers. Whether they are found or not, does not affect the biblical view of history.

The fundamental debate is really about the most trustworthy source of information about history. Do we start with the Bible,

Rock Layers

Secular history   Biblical history

which God says is true in every detail, including its history, or do we start with the changing theories of imperfect man? God tells Christians to walk by faith and that "without faith it is impossible to please Him" (Hebrews 11:6). But this is not a blind faith. God has filled the world with clear evidences that confirm the truth of His Word and the certainty of the Christian faith. The fossil record itself is an incredible testimony to the truth of God's Word and His promise to "blot out" all land dwelling, air-breathing animals and humans in a worldwide catastrophe.

1. A. Snelling, "Where are all the human fossils?" *Creation* 14(1):28–33, December, 1991; J. Morris, *The Young Earth*, Master Books, Green Forest, Arkansas, 2002, 71.

2. D. Fouts and K. Wise, "Blotting out and breaking up: miscellaneous Hebrew studies in geocatastrophism," *Proceedings of the Fourth International Conference on Creationism*, Creation Science Fellowship, Pittsburgh, 1998, 219.

3. "The Human Toll," www.tsunamispecialenvoy.org/country/humantoll.asp.

4. T. Pickett, "Population of the Pre-Flood World," www.ldolphin.org/pickett.html; H. Morris, *Biblical Cosmology and Modern Science*, Baker Book House, Grand Rapids, Michigan, 1970, 77–78; Morris, *The Young Earth*, 71.

5. D. Hinrichsen, "Coasts in Crisis," www.aaas.org/international/ehn/fisheries/hinrichs.htm.

6. J. Woodmorappe, *Studies in Flood Geology*, Institute for Creation Research, El Cajon, California, 1999, 59. This number actually comes from A.B. Ronov, "The earth's sedimentary shell," *International Geology Review* 24(11):1321–1339, 1982.

7. Morris, *The Young Earth*, 71.

8. "Where is the earth's water located?" U.S. Geological Survey, ga.water.usgs.gov/edu/earthwherewater.html.

9. L. Dicks, "The creatures time forgot," *New Scientist*, 164(2209): 36–39, October 23, 1999.

10. R. Driver, "Sea monsters . . . more than a legend?" *Creation* 19(4):38–42, September 1997.

11. www.answersingenesis.org/docs2/4416livingfossil_tree12-25-2000.asp.

12. www.pbs.org/wgbh/nova/fish/other.html.

Bodie Hodge attended Southern Illinois University at Carbondale (SIUC) and received a BS and MS (in 1996 and 1998 respectively) there in mechanical engineering. His specialty was a subset of mechanical engineering based in advanced materials processing, particularly starting powders.

Bodie conducted research for his master's degree through a grant from Lockheed Martin and developed a New Method of Production of Submicron Titanium Diboride. The new process was able to make titanium diboride cheaper, faster and with higher quality. This technology is essential for some nanotechnologies.

Currently, Bodie is a speaker, writer, and researcher in AiG's Outreach Department.

Dinosaurs: Living Large

by Marcus Ross

*I*f we're honest about it, most of us think that dinosaurs are pretty cool (at least, if the box office or all those "educational" toys are any indication). How is it that dinosaurs inspire so much devotion? After all, no one makes movies about trilobites.

When most people think about dinosaurs, they think of one word: big. But dinosaurs had a wide range in size. Some, like *Compsognathus*, were only about a foot tall, while others, like the duck-billed hadrosaurs, were bigger than SUVs. All told, it is difficult to precisely identify the average size of a dinosaur.[1]

But it is the big dinosaurs that impress us. And the biggest of them all are found among the sauropods.

Being large had its advantages. Before Adam's fall into sin, all land-dwelling, air-breathing animals ate plants (Genesis 1:30), and sauropods could graze on the higher vegetation. After Adam's sin brought evil and death into the world, being big and tall had another advantage: scaring off predators.

Biggest of the big: the sauropods

The sauropods ("lizard feet") included the largest land animals in history. With fossils on every continent, sauropods are easily recognized by their extremely long necks and tails, which are anchored to a huge body and held up by towering legs.

Familiar North American sauropods include *Apatosaurus*, *Brachiosaurus*, and *Diplodocus*. At 115 feet (35 m), *Seismosaurus*,

Illustration by Jon Taylor

the "earth shaker," is the longest land animal ever discovered, and is even longer than a blue whale! Most massive of all is *Brachiosaurus*, who tipped (or broke!) the scales at around 30 tons (27 metric tons)![2]

Being the biggest kid on the block has obvious advantages, but it also presents some huge challenges. For instance, how do you support and move all that bulk?

My, what big feet you have! And body, and neck . . .

Sauropods had an enormous chest, which housed their massive lungs, heart, and stomach. To hold up these massive bodies, the legs were giant columns of bone. The femur (upper leg bone) of *Camarasaurus* stands over 4 feet high (1.2 m) and over 1 foot wide (0.3 m), making *Camarasaurus* 10 feet tall (3 m) at its hip. Not to be outdone, *Brachiosaurus* was over 16 feet (5 m) at the shoulder. Its head towered 40 feet (12 m) above the ground.

To help support their weight, the same bones that make up the palm of our hand (metacarpals) and most of our feet (metatarsals) were organized vertically, and in a semicircle, similar to elephant feet. In effect, sauropods walked on their toes!

Another feature that set the sauropods apart from other dinosaurs was their long neck, designed for foraging food. Most sauropods held their necks out horizontal to the ground. They could swing their necks in a wide arc, allowing them to forage large areas in front of them without moving around much.

Their necks were equal to or slightly longer than their torsos. *Mamenchiasaurus*, a sauropod found in China, takes this to an extreme: its neck equals the length of the rest of the entire body! Other sauropods took a different approach to feeding. The neck of *Brachiosaurus* was angled upward, allowing it to reach high into the treetops, giving it access to food that most other animals could not reach.

Unlike many paintings and plastic toys, most sauropods did not hold their heads up high to browse on tall trees or "snorkel" under water (the pressure on their lungs and air passage would have been too great to take a breath).

The key to understanding how sauropods used their necks is their vertebrae. Think of a crane. In the center is a tower, with high-tension wires running to both ends. On a dinosaur, the tower was the hips, and muscle tendons ran from there to the head. In some species, we can see depressions in the vertebrae where they were held in place.

This design reduced the neck's range of motion, so a sauropod couldn't lift its head high or look directly backward, but it could gently sweep its head left and right without straining the muscles that kept its head off the ground. The long tails of most sauropods also helped to balance the weight of the head and neck.

From neck to tail, sauropod vertebrae are very big. So to shed a few pounds, God designed them with a lighter construction, including occasional holes or thin regions. This design is similar to modern steel construction.

What to feed a behemoth

One striking feature of sauropods is the small size of the head relative to the enormous body. How could they get enough to eat?

Sauropod teeth were often long and peg-like, designed to strip vegetation off plants; they did not chew their food. Instead, it would pass into their huge, vat-like stomach, where bacteria would help break down and ferment the vegetation until useful for food. Sauropods would also swallow rocks (called *gastroliths*) that would grind down the food. This type of digestion allowed sauropods to eat food sources (like conifers) many other plant-eaters did not.

We have little knowledge of the actual food eaten by sauropods, but the types of plants buried with them indicate low-quality, high-fiber conifers, ferns, and ginkos. One recent discovery from India gave us an unusual glimpse: some large fossilized dung (called *coprolites*), likely from sauropods, preserved several types of grasses.

They grow up so fast

Sauropods grew to enormous sizes. But how fast?

Until the late 1990s, little was known about how sauropods had their young and how fast they grew. But the discovery of a huge nesting ground in Argentina gave paleontologists a never-before-seen view into the lives of sauropods. Many nests were found, and each had multiple layers of eggs. More amazing still was that the eggs preserved skeletons of the unhatched dinosaurs. Strangely, though, no adult skeletons were found. In other rocks where sauropods are found, there are often medium-sized juveniles along with adults. Perhaps as the Flood waters were coming closer, the parents were forced to abandon the nesting site.

Based on studies of bone structures formed while the animal grew, it took about 20 years for a large sauropod to reach maturity. Their lifespan may have been 100 years or more. So while sauropods matured slower than large whales (which require only 5–6 years to reach maturity), their growth was still rather fast when we consider how huge they became. And unlike whales, which drink up to 100 gallons a day of their mother's milk in the first year, young sauropods dined on conifers, far less nutritious fare than milk.

Truly gentle giants

Sauropods were without comparison in God's creation. They were certainly the largest animals ever to walk His creation. Their very footsteps could make the ground shake. Imagine the power of a herd! As creatures made on Day Six of creation, they truly were "behemoth" ("beasts of the field" in Genesis 1:25). Made along with us, their amazing size and power should remind us of the awesome power and glory of our Lord and Creator, Jesus Christ.

---

1.   Determining the average dinosaur size isn't easy. In "Implications of Body-Mass Estimates for Dinosaurs," *Journal of Vertebrate Paleontology* 14(4): 520–33, Jan Peczkis calculated that the average size of a dinosaur was between 1 and 10 tons. Two things push this number lower: first, more small dinosaurs are being discovered than large ones (a trend noted by Peczkis, which has continued to today); second, many early methods of determining dinosaur size likely overestimated their mass. So it is likely that the average mass of a dinosaur was less than 1 ton.

2.   Much of the data in this article came from Fastovsky and Weishample, *The Evolution and Extinction of the Dinosaurs*, 2nd ed. (2005), and Weishample, Dodson, and Osmólska, *The Dinosauria*, 2nd ed. (2004).

Marcus Ross is the assistant professor of geology and assistant director for the Center for Creation Studies at Liberty University. He holds a masters in paleontology and a PhD in geosciences from the University of Rhode Island.

Dinosaur Killer

by Paul F. Taylor

The idea has been ingrained in our consciousness that dinosaurs died out because a large asteroid or comet hit the earth some 65 million years ago. So it may be a surprise to realize how recent this theory is.

Over the years dozens of theories have been proposed. When I was in school many years ago, I was taught that the shells of dinosaur eggs were becoming too thin, so they were not hatching properly. The teacher never explained why this happened only to dinosaur eggs while birds' eggs or other reptile eggs did just fine, but many people believed the theory.

K-T boundary

The impact theory first gained popularity in the 1980s. It was formulated as a result of new studies of the so-called "K-T extinction event."

To understand this theory, you need to understand the term extinction event. Whenever a number of organisms appear to be missing in a layer of rocks above another layer where they are found, evolutionary geologists call this an extinction event.

The most well-known extinction event is at the boundary between Cretaceous and Tertiary rocks. (Cretaceous rocks are indicated by a K to distinguish them from Cambrian rocks, which have a C abbreviation.) This boundary occurred 65 million years ago on the evolutionary time-scale, and dinosaurs appear only at the bottom on the Cretaceous side. Other animal species are not found above this boundary, including many marine reptiles and plants.

The father and son team of Luis and Walter Alvarez discovered that rocks from the K-T boundary have an unexpectedly high concentration of iridium. They assumed that this could not have come from earth because they assumed the earth was originally molten and any iridium would have sunk to the core after millions of years. The Alvarez team therefore suggested that this iridium came from a colliding asteroid.

In 1990, the supposed "smoking gun" of the impact theory was found. Formations at Chicxulub, Mexico, appeared to be the remnants of a very large impact crater.

GEOLOGIC TABLE: The geologic table summarizes the earth's rock layers. According to secular scientists, they record millions of years of history, but the Bible indicates that the layers were laid over the past 6,000 years.

CENOZOIC	Quaternary
	Tertiary
MESOZOIC	Cretaceous
	Jurassic
	Triassiac
PALEOZOIC	Permian
	Pennsylvanian
	Mississippian
	Devonian
	Silurian
	Ordovician
	Cambrian
PRECAMBRIAN	

THE K-T BOUNDARY: This visible boundary between two layers of strata (Cretaceous and Tertiary) is thought to be the result of a mass extinction.

Such a huge impact would have sent a large dust cloud into the atmosphere, blocking sunlight from the earth and causing some species to die out. In some variants of the theory, a comet rather than an asteroid caused the deadly impact.

But the theory has some problems. For example, some extremely light-sensitive species in the ocean did survive. Another problem is that the cloud would cause a long period of extreme cold, somewhat like the so-called "nuclear winter" that might follow the dropping of nuclear weapons.

A third problem is that there is too much iridium to fit with the theory. Although asteroids do have iridium in them, they do not normally spread out the iridium upon impact. (In other words, areas around impacts are not iridium-enriched.) In at least one case, the iridium would have taken half a million years to cover the earth, by evolutionary counting.

Far more likely is that the iridium enrichment came from volcanic activity, not outer space. Volcanoes do produce iridium and spread it out.

As a result of these and other problems, some evolutionary scientists do not accept the impact theory.

Other theories

If the impact theory is not correct, then how is the disappearance of dinosaurs to be explained? Some scientists have suggested that the world's climate suddenly became too cold. Others have suggested that their numbers declined as dinosaurs ate each other. A few theories have been wacky, such as the suggestion that dinosaurs died out from a plague of indigestion.

There is another possibility, ignored in secular science journals. While the impact theory admits the possibility of a global catastrophe resulting from an asteroid or comet, the Bible describes a very different global catastrophe that could have caused the "K-T extinction event"—the worldwide Flood of Genesis 6–9.

The Bible says that "all fountains of the great deep were broken up" (Genesis 7:11). The breakup of the earth's crust would certainly have caused volcanoes on an unprecedented scale during the Flood, explaining the iridium in the K-T boundary. The bulk of the world's fossils would have formed as a result of this catastrophe.

While pairs of every kind of dinosaur survived the Flood on board the Ark, it appears that their population never grew large in the new world. Like so many other kinds of animals, their small populations finally went extinct for a variety of reasons typical of many animals, including climate changes, diseases, decrease in food supply, and humans.

Starting with the Bible, it is easy to make sense of the mass kill of dinosaurs found in the fossil record.

Paul F. Taylor graduated with his BSc in chemistry from Nottingham University and his masters in science education from Cardiff University. Paul taught science for 17 years in a state school and served as a senior speaker for Answers in Genesis–UK.

Dinosaurs—Alive After Babel?

by Paul S. Taylor

Dinosaurs! With so many strange appendages and such great size, this group of land animals is among the most amazing and diverse ever to walk the planet. Their origin and extinction is packed with mystery and controversy.

Biblical insight

God's Word answers one mystery about dinosaurs—where they came from. Genesis reveals that God created every kind of land animal on Day Six of creation (Genesis 1:20–25; see Exodus 20:11 and John 1:3). Dinosaurs are just one of a myriad of wondrous beasts which were formed from the ground on the same day as Adam (Genesis 2:19). According to the Bible, humans and dinosaurs originally lived at the same time. They were not separated by millions of years.

We also know that dinosaurs were alive in Noah's day because the Bible indicates that every kind of land animal went on the Ark (Genesis 6:20). Furthermore, we find millions of dinosaurs buried by the Flood. So two of each kind were safe on board the Ark—at least smaller, representative specimens. God promised to save one pair of every kind of air-breathing, land-dwelling animal to repopulate the world after the Flood (Genesis 6:19–20, 7:14–16).

First-hand accounts

There are many biblical and extrabiblical clues that humans continued to have first-hand knowledge of dinosaurs after the

Flood. The Bible mentions several large, mysterious animals, although it does not describe them as dinosaurs because the term dinosauria wasn't coined until 1841 by Richard Owen.

The book of Job, written a few centuries after the Flood, leads us to believe that large dinosaurs were still alive in the lush river valleys of the Middle East. It uses the ancient name *behemoth* (bih-HEE-moth), whose original meaning has been lost. This is what appears to be ancient history's best surviving description of a dinosaur. Speaking from a whirlwind in Job 40, God mentions His greatest land animal, behemoth, created to demonstrate His awesome power. The massive, plant-eating sauropods easily fit this description, including tails that sway "like a cedar." Job's account leads us to believe that large dinosaurs were still alive after the dispersion of nations at Babel.

Since dinosaurs survived the Flood, why don't we see them today? One basic problem for post-Flood dinosaurs was environmental change, making it more difficult to find the right types and sufficient quantities of food to sustain them. Dinosaurs eventually went extinct for the same basic causes that other plants and animals have gone extinct, including environmental change and human destruction. In the end, people probably killed some of them off for meat, fame, or self-defense.

Outside of the Bible, ancient peoples around the world told of heroes who killed large, reptilian creatures. These accounts are almost as numerous as flood legends. The ancient Europeans, for example, called these monsters "dragons." They appear in art, literature, and folklore.

After researching thousands of books and ancient legends, I came to see that the most ancient stories were generally the least far-fetched and magical-sounding. These are often the most sober reports of creatures that closely match known types of dinosaurs. Generally the later legends (post-extinction) are spiced-up with bizarre mythology and superhuman deeds.

Dinosaurs of Babel?

A number of stories have come down to us from the mythology of ancient Sumer (the earliest civilization that arose in Babylonia). One of the best-preserved myths tells of the hero Gilgamesh, who decided to make a name for himself by traveling to a distant land to fell cedar trees for his city. He reached the place with fifty volunteers and discovered a huge dragon that devoured trees and reeds, was fearsome to see, and had terrible teeth. The record simply states that Gilgamesh killed the beast and cut off its head for a trophy.

A much more recent legend, from the second century BC, describes an encounter that the prophet Daniel supposedly had with a dinosaur. According to this Jewish legend, the Babylonian king wanted Daniel to worship a live dragon kept in a royal temple: "And in the same place there was a great dragon, which they of Babylon worshiped. And the king said to Daniel, 'Will you also say that this is of brass? Lo, he lives, he eats, and drinks. You cannot say that he is no living god; therefore worship him.'" Daniel declined and was able to kill the animal, proving that it was not a god. (This apocryphal story is called "Bel and the Dragon." Like so many other legends, we have no outside evidence to confirm any basis in history.)

By faith or by sight?

Did any of these ancient storytellers see live dinosaurs? It is fun to imagine that some did, but we cannot be sure which stories are based on real encounters, and which are merely stories passed down over many generations. One thing seems certain, however. It is highly unlikely that so many different people groups all over the world could dream up similar stories of beasts that closely match the animals now known as dinosaurs.

We accept the biblical descriptions of behemoth by faith—and have no need of supporting evidence to accept God's Word about this and other marvelous beasts (such as the fire-breathing leviathan of Job 41). The world's legends about dragons are simply interesting clues that may provide additional insight into the ultimate demise of these wondrous creatures after the Flood.

Job—the first book of the Bible?

Descriptions of two fantastical creatures, known as behemoth and leviathan, are found in the book of Job. The author of this book was apparently Job himself, who lived in the land of Uz (see Job 1:1). Based on the book's description of his wealth and family life, Job appears to have been a patriarch and a contemporary of Abraham. Thus, the book of Job is even older than Genesis, written many years later by Abraham's descendant, Moses.

Job was probably written in the first centuries after the worldwide Flood, soon after the Tower of Babel. If Jewish tradition is correct and we received the book through Moses, he may have received it during his years in the land of Midian (near Uz). The first eleven chapters of Genesis were probably written by Adam, Noah, the sons of Noah, and Terah, and later edited or assembled by Moses, together with his own historical writings, to form the book of Genesis.

The book of Job is filled with allusions to early life after the Tower of Babel. As Bible commentator Henry M. Morris notes, Job "contains more references to creation, the Flood and other primeval events than any book of the Bible except Genesis . . . . Remarkably, it also seems to contain more modern scientific insights than any other book of the Bible."

Paul S. Taylor is the executive director of Films for Christ (Eden Communications), a ministry focused on producing Christian media. Deeply interested in creation science, Paul conducted extensive research on dinosaurs and wrote the book *The Great Dinosaur Mystery and the Bible*. Paul is also the chief designer and editor for Christian Answers Network (christiananswers.net).

Those Not-so-dry Bones

by Marcus Ross

Scientific debates often can be rather dry, filled with unfamiliar terms and minute details difficult for the lay reader to follow. But over the last five years, a shocking discovery has taken center stage in an intense debate that even children can follow. Soft, unfossilized blood vessels and red blood cells have been discovered in dinosaur fossils! How could soft tissues survive after being buried in rock?

In 2005, a team of scientists led by paleontologist Mary Schweitzer published a paper in which they described an unusual femur (upper leg bone) of a *Tyrannosaurus rex*.[1] While the outer bone was completely fossilized, the interior regions were somehow sealed off from fossilizing fluids. Inside the *T. rex* femur were intact blood vessels and red blood cells. Once freed from the bones, the blood vessels could be stretched—and even snapped back into place!

The paper produced a storm of media and scientific attention. At issue: the *T. rex* fossil is believed by evolutionists to be 68 *million* years old. How could these biological structures survive intact?

Shortly after, Schweitzer and her colleagues made more headlines with a second paper. This one described intact proteins from the *T. rex* femur.[2] The problem: laboratory tests and theoretical research have shown that proteins similar to those seen in the *T. rex* fossil degrade too quickly—even in ideal laboratory conditions—to survive for more than a few thousand years.[3]

In 2008, a paper by paleontologist Thomas Kaye and colleagues challenged Schweitzer's original findings at their core.[4] These researchers had discovered similar soft structures in a whole range of other fossil animals, including several from the same geologic layers as the *T. rex* (the Hell Creek Formation). Instead of vertebrate blood vessels and cells, this paper documented that all the structures were formed by *bacteria* some time after fossilization happened.

For example, the "stretchy" blood vessels in their samples were actually tough films, secreted by bacteria. These films looked like blood vessels because the bacteria had coated the holes where the blood vessels once were, leaving behind false "blood vessels." Kaye's team also discovered inside these bacterial "vessels" round pyrite (fool's gold) crystals. They concluded that Schweitzer's team must have mistaken these for red blood cells (which are round in reptiles and birds, but flattened in mammals). They also discovered similar kinds of organic chemicals as Schweitzer's team, but from substances made by bacteria. Kaye's paper seemed to counter most of the Schweitzer team's evidence that they had found original *T. rex* tissues.

But in early 2009, Schweitzer and colleagues struck again with a new paper.[5] Now a duck-billed dinosaur from the Judith River Formation (below the Hell Creek, and supposedly 80 million years old) was described with a host of soft-tissue structures. Furthermore, the analyses of this fossil were done by multiple, independent labs. Several vertebrate-specific proteins (collagen, elastin, and hemoglobin) were discovered, as were unambiguous osteocytes (bone-forming cells seen only in vertebrate animals).

The Schweitzer team's latest paper clearly answers all the challenges posed by Kaye's bacterial-origin hypothesis.[6] In both of Schweitzer's reports, the claim of dinosaur soft tissue is real.

But this still leaves the bigger question: how could soft tissues survive for millions of years? No experimental results support long-age survival, as the last paper by Schweitzer's team readily admits. And honestly, no young-earth creationists expected soft tissue to be found in dinosaurs. Perhaps that expectation was an artifact of our training (which is often in evolution-dominated schools). Sometimes evolutionary assumptions are in places we haven't recognized.

Yet the discovery really makes sense if the bones were buried only a few thousand years ago during Noah's Flood. One thing is for sure: more creationists will be looking inside more bones to see what treasures are hidden there.

1. M. H. Schweitzer, et al., "Soft-Tissue Vessels and Cellular Preservation in Tyrannosaurus rex," *Science* 307:1952–1955.

2. M. H. Schweitzer, et al., "Analyses of Soft Tissue from Tyrannosaurus rex Suggest the Presence of Protein," *Science* 316:277–280.

3. C. Nielsen-Marsh, "Biomolecules in Fossil Remains: A Multidisciplinary Approach to Endurance," *The Biochemist*, June 2002, pp. 12–14.

4. T. G. Kaye, et al., "Dinosaurian Soft Tissues Interpreted as Bacterial Biofilms," *PLoS One* 3(7): e2808.

5. M. H. Schweitzer, et al., "Biomolecular Characterization and Protein Sequences of the Campanian Hadrosaur B. canadensis," *Science* 234:626–631.

6. The material discovered by Kaye's team does appear to be bacterial, not vertebrate in origin. So we have evidence of both dinosaur and bacterial products, but in different fossils.

Without a Leg to Stand On

by A. P. Galling

Birds are the modern version of dinosaurs," declare many evolutionists who believe theropod dinosaurs evolved into birds.[1] Artists even go so far as to depict these reptiles with feathers and other avian features.[2] But not all evolutionists accept the dogma. In a recent *Journal of Morphology* paper, Devon Quick and John Ruben of Oregon State University exposed a major flaw in the dinosaur-to-bird model—and simultaneously revealed a unique feature of bird biology.[3]

The scientists examined the unusual way that birds use their femur (thigh bone) when walking. Unlike most other creatures, birds do not move their femurs significantly. Instead, birds use their lower legs. But their odd "knee running" motion isn't just a funny quirk. It's actually crucial to their ability to breathe rapidly. The femur bones and thigh muscles support the bird's air-sac lung as it breathes, preventing the lungs from collapsing.

"This is fundamental to bird physiology," Quick said. "It's really strange that no one realized this before."

Dinosaur fossils show no evidence of fixed femurs, the researchers determined. "Theropod dinosaurs had a moving femur and therefore could not have had a lung that worked like that in birds," Ruben explained. "That undercuts a critical piece of supporting evidence for the dinosaur–bird link." The lung structure and physiology of dinosaurs was likely much closer to crocodilian creatures than to birds.

David Menton, a former Washington University anatomist who has researched the dinosaur-to-bird idea, commented, "It appears that both feathers and the avian mode of breathing are unique to birds."

Perhaps the dinosaur–bird connection, now rejected by creationists and some evolutionists, will one day fall out of favor entirely. But Ruben noted, "There's a lot of museum politics involved in this, a lot of careers committed to a particular point of view even if new scientific evidence raises questions."

At the very least, we now know of another ingenious anatomical feature that the Creator gave birds from the very beginning so they could achieve the miracle of flight.

1. http://www.livescience.com/strangenews/090604-lost-world-dinosaurs.html.

2. http://www.ucmp.berkeley.edu/diapsids/saurischia/dromaeosauridae.html.

3. http://www3.interscience.wiley.com/journal/122395783/abstract.

A.P. Galling earned his bachelor's degree in political science from Miami University in Oxford, Ohio. He writes regularly for the Answers in Genesis website and contributes to the weekly column "News to Note."

Dinosaurs are Found in a Field of Judgment

Dinosaurs have captured the imagination of people for thousands of years. Ancient peoples imagined battles of giants where fossils were found and the bones were used as medicines. Today, massive skeletons are enshrined in museums and patrons stand in awe under the remains of these massive beasts from the past.

Placards tell the age of the fossils, where they were found, what they probably ate, and other interesting details. In order to understand dinosaurs, we have to study the fossils. This means that there is a lot of interpretation that happens. Contrary to the cliché, evidence doesn't speak for itself. A fossil toe bone can't tell us how old it is or how it helped the dinosaur it came from to walk. Evidence must be interpreted. If we are honest, we have to admit that people's view of the world influences the way they interpret data.

It is most popular today to believe that animals on the earth evolved over billions of years by random processes. When scientists who believe in evolutionary philosophy look at the fossils, they see bones from animals that lived millions of years ago. Their interpretation is colored by their prior commitment to the concepts of evolution.

Another interpretation of the evidence comes from a biblical perspective. The opening chapters of Genesis describe how God created the earth and the life that inhabited it. The account in the Bible is in direct opposition to the evolutionary view of the origin of various living things. There are many who try to reconcile the two, but you must abandon critical points of one view over the other to make them mesh. In doing so, harm is done to one or the other—if not both.

While the evolutionary interpretation sees fossils formed gradually over millions of years as life evolved, the Bible presents a starkly different view. Dinosaurs were part of the original creation described in Genesis. As land animals they would have been created on Day Six of the Creation Week, alongside the first man and woman. The formation of their fossils came during the catastrophic events of the Flood recorded in Genesis 6–9.

The Flood was a response by God to the wickedness of His creation.

> Then the LORD saw that the wickedness of man was great in the earth, and that every intent of the thoughts of his heart was only evil continually. And the LORD was sorry that He had made man on the earth, and He was grieved in His heart. So the LORD said, "I will destroy man whom I have created from the face of the earth, both man and beast, creeping thing and birds of the air, for I am sorry that I have made them." Genesis 6:5–7

The Flood was a judgment by God on a world that had rebelled against Him and His commands. As their loving Creator, God was grieved at their rebellion but His justice demanded a punishment. When we find dinosaurs fossilized they are generally in layers that were deposited by the global Flood. Rather than a record of progress, dinosaur fossils should remind us that God the Creator is serious about obedience to the laws He gives to His creation. Because God is just, He must punish disobedience.

Disobedience to God's commands is called sin. The Bible plainly talks about how sin came into the world through the disobedience of Adam and Eve and that mankind is now subject to sin. The penalty for sin is death and no person can escape that penalty. Beyond physical death, God will demand an eternal payment for sins in hell. Are you guilty of sinning against God by breaking His commands?

The Bible calls for people to examine themselves in light of God's laws. Have you ever taken anything that doesn't belong to you? Have you desired things that belong to others? Have you manipulated and lied to people? Have you lusted after others? Have you always put God first in your life?

Those are just a few of the Ten Commandments—a summary of God's commands. If you are honest with yourself, you are guilty of breaking God's laws on many occasions. If you were to stand before God, He would have to declare your guilt and punish you for your sins—bad news by any account.

But what if there were good news? What if God showed mercy to His creation?

That is what He did during the Flood for a man who trusted God.

> So the LORD said, "I will destroy man whom I have created from the face of the earth, both man and beast, creeping thing and birds of the air, for I am sorry that I have made them." But Noah found grace in the eyes of the LORD. Genesis 6:7–8

Noah was saved from the wrath that God poured out in judgment of the wickedness on the earth. He and his family were saved aboard the Ark. God has also provided a way to be saved from the wrath that is to come in the final judgment of all mankind.

We could never live a perfect life (a life without sin), so God sent an advocate for us. Jesus Christ came to earth as God in the flesh to live a life of perfect obedience. He then died on the Cross taking the punishment of sin upon himself—the innocent punished for the guilty. He then rose from the grave demonstrating His conquest over death. To all of those who will humble themselves in repentance before God and put their trust in Christ as their Lord and

Savior, God will see them innocent as Christ has already paid the punishment for their sins. Those who cling to their sins and reject what Christ has done will face God's wrath eternally.

If you will recognize the sin in your life and its offensive nature before God and turn from it, God will grant you a pardon through faith in what Christ has done. He will then give you a new life and you will not have to fear His judgment.

> [Christ] then would have had to suffer often since the foundation of the world; but now, once at the end of the ages, He has appeared to put away sin by the sacrifice of Himself. And as it is appointed for men to die once, but after this the judgment, so Christ was offered once to bear the sins of many. To those who eagerly wait for Him He will appear a second time, apart from sin, for salvation. Hebrews 9:26–28

Next time you look at a fossil, remember that it represents God's judgment on the earth. The Just Judge will judge the earth again, but His mercy is offered to you as a free gift.

> "For God so loved the world that He gave His only begotten Son, that whoever believes in Him should not perish but have everlasting life. For God did not send His Son into the world to condemn the world, but that the world through Him might be saved. He who believes in Him is not condemned; but he who does not believe is condemned already, because he has not believed in the name of the only begotten Son of God. And this is the condemnation, that the light has come into the world, and men loved darkness rather than light, because their deeds were evil. For everyone practicing evil hates the light and does not come to the light, lest his deeds should be exposed. But he who does the truth comes to the light, that his deeds may be clearly seen, that they have been done in God." John 3:16–21